I0759792

Praise for *Ancestors*

"Elegant, powerful, and relentlessly prophetic, *Ancestors* should be required reading for anyone committed to building a better self and world. Rev. William H. Lamar IV's deeply perceptive observations and beautiful prose will make you think deeply about the ways those who have moved on are still with us in ways that can be both liberating and oppressive."

—Adam Russell Taylor, author of *A More Perfect Union*

"William H. Lamar IV reminds us of the power of learning the lessons of history through discernible and intimate voices. *Ancestors* affirms the profound influence the past has on us, individually and collectively, for good and for bad. And Lamar teaches us how to choose. With keen reflections on scripture and his personal history, Reverend Lamar offers a bold primer on practicing moral imagination by leaning into the wisdom of ancestral spaces—our grandmothers, grandfathers, great uncles and aunts, and all the cloud of witnesses who continue to watch over us and speak to us, if we dare to listen. Their voices create a collective wisdom we need to hear now more than ever. Preach, preacher!"

—Liz Walker, author of *No One Left Alone*

"In *Ancestors*, Rev. William H. Lamar IV offers us more than a book—he delivers a sacred reckoning. With prophetic clarity and pastoral depth, interspersed with personal anecdotes, Lamar calls us to listen to voices that have been buried by empire but never silenced. He resurrects memory not as nostalgia, but as a revolutionary force—a living archive of Black resistance, faith, and wisdom that can guide us toward justice today. Like the prophets of old, he refuses to separate spirituality from struggle. *Ancestors* is a clarion call for those who believe that faith must confront poverty, racism, and violence with the full power of our spiritual inheritance. I am deeply moved and challenged by this work."

—Rev. Dr. Liz Theoharis, editor of *We Pray Freedom: Liturgies and Rituals from the Freedom Church of the Poor*

ANCESTORS

ANCESTORS

THOSE WHO BLESS US, CURSE US, AND HOLD US

WILLIAM H. LAMAR IV

Broadleaf Books
Minneapolis

ANCESTORS
Those Who Bless Us, Curse Us, and Hold Us

32 31 30 29 28 27 26 25 1 2 3 4 5 6 7 8 9

Library of Congress Control Number: 2025023785 (print) | 2025023786 (ebook)

Cover image and design: Kristin Miller

Print ISBN: 978-1-5064-8221-7
eBook ISBN: 978-1-5064-8222-4

Printed in India.

CONTENTS

INTRODUCTION

AUNT VINEY WAS the first ancestor to reach out for me. She beckoned me from an old, oval frame that failed in its attempt to control her energy. I knew she was dead. She had to be. Her picture was probably the oldest thing I had seen. I was attracted by her mystery yet frightened by the chasm between us. The years and experiences that separated us surely made her unknowable to me and me unknowable to her. But I *wanted* to know her. And I felt her beckoning me, wanting to know little Billy Lamar. Decades earlier she had saved my grandmother from so much pain. And I somehow understood she was my saving too.

Ancestors can show up in conspicuous places. Aunt Vincy's picture held court in my maternal grandmother's—Nanny's—home, hanging in the most prominent place in the house. From my vantage point as a toddler she was high and lifted up. I would cut my eyes toward her as I walked out of the house. And it seemed like she was cutting her eyes toward me, too.

Though it felt taboo, I worked up the nerve to ask Nanny who the woman in the frame was. She told me, also assuaging my fear. She said, "Nothing in this house will hurt you, Billy." I still believe that.

We both looked at the picture together. Aunt Viney, she said, took in Nanny and her sister Susie Bell and raised them as her own when Nanny's parents died. Aunt Viney showed overwhelming hospitality to and sacrificed for her nieces. She became their mother. She chose them. And Nanny revered her.

Nanny, an artist, seamstress, floral arranger, was a queen of creation. She strategically and deliberately hung Aunt Viney's picture in the center of it all. It was as if that picture was the pillar that bore the weight of the house and our lives.

Aunt Viney reigned at the front door to remind Nanny of her ancestral debt. And to teach little Billy and all of us where we came from and who we were expected to become. Her eyes followed us with interest and wisdom: We were to open our hearts, our homes, and our minds. We were to remember that life can be hard, but a way can be made. We were to try, with everything in us, to create spaces where harm had no dominion.

A few years ago my mother gave me Aunt Viney's picture. When it is restored, I will hang it in a place of prominence in my home. Aunt Viney has lessons yet to teach her niece's grandson. Though I was hesitant to meet her gaze, Nanny taught me to lean into ancestral space. And since that moment, ancestral space has continued to be a refreshing oasis.

* * *

A colleague and I had an interesting conversation recently. We talked big things—theology, spirituality, politics, economics.

We talked granular things—budgets, buildings, human resources, technology. Both of us try our best to remember that the granular things are not separate from the big things. Together, the big and small work to produce the possibility of transformation in individuals and communities. We tried to thread that needle as our conversation oscillated between kvetching, commiseration, and encouragement.

We laughed about the signs of hope in our contexts. And we laughed about the intractable, energy-draining stuff that we just couldn't fix. When my colleague asked me how I dealt with those realities, I shared my practice of leaning into ancestral space. Inviting, listening, looking, and waiting for those who came before us to journey with us, to teach us what can be taught, and to make us aware of that which remains hidden. My colleague gave me a flat look. Her abrupt response to my suggestion jars me still. "My ancestors," she said, "can't help me. They are the problem."

Our ancestral experiences could not have been more different.

And that's what this book is about. Whether we invite ancestors to journey with us or not, they are walking ahead of us, beside us, and behind us. They are pulling us, pushing us, and sometimes restraining us. Whether we are aware of it or not, ancestors are still speaking, some quite loudly, and even if we pretend not to hear we cannot not hear. Some may never admit it, but we are all searching for ancestors, even as ancestors are surely searching for us. Where we are imprisoned as individuals and societies, ancestors are our most skilled jailers. Where we are free, ancestors are at the vanguard of our liberation.

My colleague was acutely aware that the ancestors who came before us exercise a spiritual influence over our imaginations and our ethics. She knew that moving her entrenched community in a different direction would cause the living to entreat the dead for resources to keep the status quo in place.

Whenever we move closer to the flourishing of creation and shared human abundance, whenever the lie of scarcity suffers a potential mortal wound, the living call upon legions of ancestors whose images and words and symbols keep us locked in the politics of death. This discourse between the living and the dead animates our popular culture, journalism, art, politics, scholarship, commerce, preaching, and teaching.

From the particularity of my vocation as a pastor, I encounter the universality of the human condition. I rejoice with people during times of jubilation—marriages, births, graduations, housewarmings, baptisms, and new employment. Rarely have I shared these moments without those individuals joyfully invoking ancestors. They shed tears and smile broadly when remembering parents, grandparents, spouses, or siblings. They speak a wish that someone who has ascended to the ancestral realm could be present now to share and to celebrate. They see and experience the ongoing presence of ancestors in the faces of infants and in the laughter and body language of the elders.

At times of death and grief, I have seen people cling to ancestors to survive shadowy nights of the soul. Those in transit from life to death see and have conversations with family members and friends who had pierced the veil decades ago. I have witnessed this. It is real. The dying have asked me if I could see or hear the ancestral host coming to escort them to the next realm.

I have yet to see what they see or hear what they hear. What is being revealed to them remains hidden from us for now. But I know what I don't see as the dying often point to and extend their hands to embrace the physicality of the ancestral realm. I write this book about leaning into ancestral space, because this is not just a head trip or spiritual journey. Ancestors beckon our limbs, our loves, and our very lives—sometimes for good and, as the look in my colleague's eyes reminds me, sometimes for ill.

Ancestors remind me I am caught up in G-d's dream of a new heaven and a new earth. All things are being made new now. Rising out of scripture, Mary's song, which samples Hannah's song, rings true. G-d is deposing tyrants. G-d is filling the hungry with good things and sending the greedy away empty. But resistance to this eschatological dream comes from forces arrayed against shared abundance among human beings and against the flourishing of creation. I see these forces made visible when I engage in protests against harm to my community, organize people for justice. I saw them when I was arrested and jailed for trying to make real the promise of democracy, and when I have prayed with those whose bones are being crushed by the brutalities of our present sociopolitical order.

These forces are embodied; they have taken on flesh. They stand against what is human. They are at war with the divine. They hoard. They steal. They kill.

There's no self-righteousness, here. Naming my complicity in the very systems I abhor, I have asked myself why do people fight against what is just and fair and beautiful? Why do we insist on extracting life from the land and from our siblings without giving thought to their replenishment and rejuvenation? How did we get trapped in the logic of death? Is there an escape?

These questions return me to neglected aspects of my faith. I was taught to affirm my belief in the communion of saints, a mystical idea that the living and the dead remain connected palpably, yet inscrutably. I was taught that we are surrounded by a great cloud of witnesses. Those who have trod our path watch us and cheer us.

But the wisdom of the ages teaches us that where there is light there is also shadow. If there were a Christian version of midrash, a wise divine would have long ago asserted that the cloud of witnesses also contains those who jeer us and trip us. We run on anyhow, as Jesse Owens ran. Knowing that the enemies of humanity are in the stands may help us run farther and faster.

Some in the human family are experiencing cultural tremors and some are experiencing cultural earthquakes, but all are being tossed and unmoored from the meaning-making myths that define us. And we run, knowing ancestors have run before, helping us run on. A culture will never surpass the theological, moral, social, or political imagination of the ancestors whose names they call and whose stories they tell. The multifaceted malaise experienced in the imperial United States and around the globe is as much a crisis of identity and narrative as it is anything that can be quantified by the social sciences or illumined by the natural sciences.

What is required in this time—what is paramount—for our changing personal and national narratives is imagination. Can we envision new ways of ordering our lives and our communities? Are we stuck in the now, or can we dance into a more just and beautiful future? How is seeing beyond the present nurtured and actualized? Is our reality bound to the present, or can we live in and learn from the past and the future amid our now moment?

I do not have many answers, but I am certain that life on our precious planet depends upon our taking this interrogation seriously. And taking the role of ancestors seriously. That's what this book is about.

Our spiritual, moral, social, and political imaginations are inextricably bound to the ancestors whose names we call and whose stories we tell. The imagination needed to think and to pray and to act ourselves into something different depends on those whose lives, though they be dead, continue to form the contours of our individual and collective existence.

* * *

Ancestors are not just those from whom we may be directly descended. And ancestors are not just those to whom we are related by blood. Ancestors are those who are no longer physically present, but whose energy, radiance, and/or shadow continue to pierce our reality in life-giving or death-dealing ways.

Ancestors, like living humans, contain the spark of the divine. They are beings beyond our creation and control. From African cultures I have learned of the sublime notion of G-d as the great and primary ancestor, as James Weldon Johnson's poetic vision explores. Creating us all is a maternal and paternal Being who desires fellowship with humans. Our ancestors, those radiant and those shadowy, find their origin in this One.

When we call our ancestors' names, we are not just speaking them. We are reinscribing limits or transgressing boundaries. We are arousing death or summoning life. When we tell our ancestors' stories we are rediscovering and traveling upon well-worn paths and escorting younger generations, for good or for ill, along with us.

We choose our ancestors. We choose the names we call. And we are clear about the names we will not call, names that curse us, names that will never bless us.

We choose the stories of ancestors we tell. Some are damned or damnable lies. Some move us closer to the safe shores of abundance and a thriving humanity and a vibrant earth.

We speak of the ancestors whose names and stories can bring us life, but we understand the merchants of death seek to erase and to disappear them. There are ancestors whose onslaught of death has continued unabated though their bones rest in G-d's good earth. They will ride on, but they cannot have dominion.

And ancestors choose us. We must learn how to grasp those who hold life and how to let others go.

As we choose our ancestors, too, may we claim those committed to life and not to the status quo. May the names we call and the stories we tell make us more human and more aware of the divinity resident in each of us—past, present, and future.

1

A Crisis of Identity

I STOOD ON the high diving board at the recreation center in East Macon, Georgia, where I took swimming lessons. It was time for the final test. I had checked every other box: I could float face down and on my back. I could tread water like a terrier. I swam the length of the pool (not elegantly, but with minimal splashing). My nine-year-old hands were cupped, my kicks were firm, and my head swiveled as I chased oxygen and the pool's edge. In that order.

I have never been an athlete. I was the kid who struck out at T-ball. But my parents were wise enough to make me live in my body. I was good with words and ideas, but hesitant to engage physically. I did not want to make mistakes. I did not want my dropped ball or strikeout to cost my team the game. I did not want to run around the field with boys who lapped my lethargic best effort. Let Billy talk. Let Billy read. Don't give Billy the ball. I was thrilled when it was my time to read aloud in Sunday school or in school. And I was petrified when it was my turn at bat.

My parents sensed this. And I did get better at baseball. They knew I needed the camaraderie of peers and to learn the joys and burdens of teamwork. Toward the end of my short-lived Little League career, I was hitting the ball with some power. Still, too many cats stole second base as I crouched catching painful fastballs from a dude with an arm like a cannon.

My grandmother Sallie loved baseball. I can still see her nodding off after a hard day's work as we sat and watched the Atlanta Braves. Sharing those moments with her was sheer joy. She and her sister, Aunt Babe, knew the players and statistics. They lit up when talking about the game. But swimming. Not. At. All. The thought of swimming chilled Sallie.

I have long speculated about my grandmother's aversion to swimming. It is not just her. Many of the elders I knew who have traveled into mystery were opposed to themselves or anyone they loved getting near bodies of water big or small. Some of that fear seemed to verge on irrationality. One family reunion I recall my uncle and aunt were apoplectic that their grandchildren even went near a plastic kiddie pool on a smoldering July afternoon.

Water is a site of terror for Black people. The Middle Passage—the Maafa—is a water-soaked and living remembrance. Too many of us met our demise when water overcame us by the design of the murderous. I cannot know what memory water held for my grandmother—even if I had thought to ask, I would have been afraid to. Likely I would have opened up an emotional portal deeply painful for her, and overwhelming the child that I was.

Maybe my grandmother, whom we joyfully called Mommee, knew what Toni Morrison knew. No, she certainly knew it: what Morrison called water's perfect memory and how it always returns to where it used to be. What we call floods are simply water remembering and returning. It was the memory of the water, of where water might return to, that was more than likely what was too much for Mommee.

But my mother wanted her children to know how to swim. She didn't just want that. She demanded that against the desires of her mother-in-law and probably others related to her. Then as now, my mother's determination was and is a marvel of nature. With grace and style—and by other means if pushed—my extraordinary mother makes magic happen for her family and her community.

My swim coach was treading water in the deep end of the pool, waiting for me. He shouted up, "Jump, Billy!" My friends were around. The ones who had already jumped registered mixed sentiments. Some were encouraging. Some jeered. I remember the jeerers by name. My body quivered. My voice quavered. I don't remember what I said to my coach. I don't want to remember. Forty years later I am embarrassed.

Our families were there for the final test. I was afraid to jump, and I was too embarrassed to walk back down the board a failure. I saw my mother. Then when I looked again I didn't. I felt something vibrating around me on the board. The rhythm of the footsteps was familiar. I had heard that music before. Mama had climbed the high diving board. She pushed me into the water.

I would probably still be on that board, frozen by fear, if my mother had not loved me enough to push me into the water. The same holy woman who pushed me into this beautiful and broken world from the water of her body now pushed me into the uncertain waters of the pool. The stakes were relatively low in a swimming class in a public park. Safety measures abounded. But the waters roiling around us in this moment and beckoning us to jump in and do something offer no guarantee of survival.

For me, for all of us who stand above the waterline, now is not the time to stand on that board looking down at the destruction swirling all around us. Institutions that we once counted on are being hollowed out. Laws and rules of engagement long respected are flouted and broken with bravado and bellicosity. And the most vulnerable among us, who live downstream from these decisions, are losing the very substance that held their fragile existences together.

My ancestors sang of the baptism required: "Wade in the water / Wade in the water, children / Wade in the water / God's gonna trouble the water." The Divine is a water-troubler, stirring and churning and heating the water until hatred, injustice, and avarice boil away. You and I are called to join the waters as co-troublers. It is not enough to talk about the water and write about the water. We must jump in and join G-d in troubling it.

From the very beginnings water called us. The Genesis text gives us a beautiful image. In the primordial moments before creation, the Divine interacts with water. The verb that describes G-d and water's interaction can be translated as hovered over, brooded over, swept over, or reclined into. The Divine dwells and plays in and around the water. And G-d never allows the water to rest for very long. Rivers run and streams trickle and oceans roar. Our work is to join G-d's divine waterworks and take our place as cocreators of the world the divine intends.

The water is deep, and it is fear inducing. I know. I am the guy who was so afraid to get in the water that my mother pushed me in. And here is the pearl. My mother knew that my vocation was to enter the water. That calling is one I share with all people who want a new world to emerge. Those of faith traditions similar to my own must stop petitioning for divine intervention when we are called to jump—or have a kindly, determined one push us in. As the Rev. K. Mekhi Jackson writes in his article "The Call for a Radical Black Christian Church," we "must stop waiting on divine intervention and instead become the divine intervention." That is what G-d has been praying for since we took our first steps as beings made in the image and likeness of the divine.

My mother knew that ancestors were in the water waiting for me. Whenever and wherever we jump, they are waiting to receive us. To show us the way. To take us to vessels of safety upon the sea and to let us know when it is time to jump in and swim again.

The swimming is getting more dangerous. Yet, we are called to swim, to exert individual and communal effort, in waters teeming with dangers and challenges. We cannot tread water. To tread water is to accept what is. Too often we exert energy simply keeping our heads above water. Treading water is physically taxing but you get nowhere fast. You survive, but we were not created to survive. We were created to thrive and to trouble waters designed to steal our humanity and the radiant spark of the divine that dwells in us all.

My ancestors did not sing of accepting the water. They sang of G-d's troubling it. We are born troubling the waters of our mother's womb. We break into the world soon after the water breaks. We do not come here in peace. We are pushed from womb water into the roiling waters of life.

We will never accept our way out of the myriad challenges that afflict us. I appreciate the motto attributed to Hannibal, "I will find a way or make one." Too many of us, crushed by capitalism's robbery and cheapening of our time and spiritually malnourished by what passes as theology in America, simply accept what is. I don't know how successful I have been at changing things or even changing myself, but I was not raised to accept things as they are. I don't think that G-d would waste creative energy on us if we were destined to simply observe the world as it is. We are cocreators with G-d of worlds of justice, peace, and liberation for our bodies, souls, and communities. We cannot accept what is. We wade in the water. We swim upstream and against currents. Our troubling of the water changes the water, and it changes us.

Our jumping in and swimming is not an act of acceptance. My mother pushed me into the water because I needed her unsolicited, yet necessary help to move beyond fear. Fear keeps us trembling on the high diving board. The water howls at us, taunts us, and seeks to bully us. It dares us to jump in. To trouble the water is to trouble ourselves. The human body is composed mainly of water. Fear of water is fear of self. Fear of possibility. Fear of cocreation. Fear of human power.

We are water. To say that the water must be troubled is to say that we must be troubled. We will not accept the evil we do to one another. We will not accept devaluing and destroying human life for power and profit. We will jump in and trouble the water. Is the water dangerous? Yes. But the danger my people have faced since coming to this strange, brutal land has not kept us paralyzed. We swim and create beauty. We swim and build community. We swim and demand justice. We do not accept the water as it is.

Some will wade and some will jump but we are all called into the waters of our present moment just as we were called from the waters of the womb. To enter the water is an act of interrogation and exploration. Why does this water stand between us and liberation? How can we get through it together? How will the water change if we own our power to survive and thrive as we navigate it together?

A strange thing happened when I was pushed into the water. I learned to trust my own buoyancy. There is always an upward force exerted upon one immersed in water. Buoyancy is ancestral energy. It pushes us powerfully to the surface when the water wants to take us under. When in the deepest of water, I have felt ancestors pulling me, guiding me. They are expert navigators. Those of us who have survived the water know of their encompassing, luminous presence. There is nothing like knowing that we never swim alone.

We swim because we cannot accept where we are. We swim for a farther, peaceful shore that we can inhabit together. We question the world as it is with each stroke. We will never accept our way out of the morass of the present age. Nothing will come of staring down at the water in fear. We may be able, however, to question our way out. Questions reorient us; they reposition us in the water. When we interrogate ourselves and our condition, we occupy space both within our challenges and outside of them. We begin to imagine and thus cocreate our desired peaceful shore with our water-troubling G-d.

* * *

We enter this wondrous world as curious little creatures born of water, full of questions, and seeing beyond "what is." Children incessantly ask the questions adults won't. They begin with *why*. They are miniature philosophers and theologians demanding to know why people die and where G-d lives and why the water is so foreboding. Curiosity leads us to the water's edge. It leads us up the high diving board. With the help of G-d and the ancestors, curiosity will lead us into the water and buoyancy will keep us from being swallowed by it. The peril of the water is real.

To nurture our natural human curiosity is the debt the mature owe the young. My parents blessedly made space for my questions. I fried their nerves, but they did not dam the waters of my inquisitiveness. Yes, they had to keep mop and bucket at the ready because those waters frequently overflowed. I asked strangers embarrassing questions about themselves. I held family members and friends hostage with weapons of mass intrusiveness. My beleaguered parents sought psychological assistance just in case something was amiss. They were told that I was being me and that if they aggressively hindered my behavior I would not flourish, and we would all regret it. I am indebted to my parents for their own inquisitiveness and seeking of answers, now and always.

As I reflect now, I believe that we all have the predisposition of the young. We ask questions. We probe. We ponder. We don't accept things as they are. We want to know why. We make bold statements. But our family, our theological, political, and economic systems hold back the waters of our inquiry. This inculcates fear of troubling waters. This keeps us from embracing the revolutionary work of our water-troubling G-d.

* * *

Those who control these systems are consumed with the maintenance of present power relationships. They teach us, implicitly and explicitly, to conform, keep quiet, put our heads down, and to keep staring helplessly at the unjust waters they churn to petrify us and to make us afraid. Even when Spirit calls us to wade in, we clock in and we clock out day after day, going about our widget making and refusing to breach the water's edge.

One of the gifts Black ancestors bequeathed to me and to any who would know the truth is a healthy skepticism of the American empire and its rhetoric. We have always known that this nation's commitment to democracy was contingent upon race, gender, wealth, and the whims of those who control the political class. We see that now more than ever. The fact that freedom for many in America is different from the dictionary's definition of freedom is written upon the flesh of my forebears and their descendants.

The US Senate is where democracy goes to die. In a split chamber, legislation that should move us toward equity, justice, and care for the earth dies in an upper chamber designed to ensure the tyranny of the minority.

In 1982 my parents' voting rights were more protected than their grandchildren's voting rights are now. The Voting Rights Act of 1965 was eviscerated by the Supreme Court's white supremacist decision to allow states with bloody records of disenfranchising Black people and others to sidestep federal preclearance of their voter suppression shenanigans. Is this democracy? We know the answer. We cheer on kakistocracy as it parades in democratic garb. This does not have to be.

Communities of faith have capitulated to capitalist logic. They support people and ideas that shrink our sense of connectedness and shared responsibility. They cheer the accumulation of power and wealth as G-d's will while punishing anyone and anything that would share the wealth of the planet and the nations with all people. I hesitate to speak outside of my own milieu, but I see signs of theological surrender to the gods of the status quo all around us. Even prophetic and progressive Christians have bought what has been sold by those who would neutralize the revolutionary potential of the gospel. Faith has been privatized on the left and on the right: prisons, schools, health care, and warfare. We have been shaped not to trouble the water.

We are being theologically atomized. Grand cosmic visions of G-d's new heaven and new earth have been shrunk to fit only in individual human hearts. And this smallness, this disconnection, leaves us to fend for ourselves, without a compelling story to link our desires and our destinies with the Divine. We know that in too many cases, faith has become the servant of the wealthy and the powerful. They co-opt signs, symbols, and language to dupe the masses into thinking the powerful carry the imprimatur of the Divine. We are aware that this is neither our story nor our song. Yet, our lack of a robust response is a form of acceptance. This does not have to be.

Our local communities are microcosms of our global reality. One side of town flourishes with stately homes, tree-covered boulevards, verdant parks, and state-of-the-art schools. The other side of town languishes as food deserts, over-policing, lack of public transportation, and crumbling schools and infrastructure drain resources and life. Those suffering in this arrangement are not less fortunate nor are they under-resourced. We must dispense with these euphemisms if we want to be made well.

Recent scholarship documents that these people have been dehumanized and victimized by violent public policy and racist and classist political activity. Savagery stemming from economic envy and lynching terrorized these communities well into the twentieth century. Those who led economically and politically were killed, bombed out, and threatened. Urban renewal and the building of highways and roads destroyed businesses and razed homes. Schools and other vital infrastructure never received the public support enjoyed by the white and the wealthy. Redlining crippled the free flow of capital. Restrictive covenants concentrated poverty and limited opportunity.

Homes in certain areas are seriously undervalued, not because of the quality of the homes, but because of the complexion of the owners and the neighbors. All the while these people pay taxes only to see their funds siphoned off to keep the other side of town beautiful. This practice continues and we are living with the legacy of these decisions. No, these people are not less fortunate. They are victims of political violence. They are not under-resourced; they are being robbed. Why won't we equitably allocate public dollars in our communities? Why do we value some people and places while leaving others to fend for themselves? I am convinced that we are more likely to be transformed if we begin in our cities, towns, and villages. But most of us accept these injustices quietly. This water must be troubled.

When asking the necessary questions about how we came to be where we are as a nation, as communities of faith, and as localities, I became frustrated. Empirical evidence abounds: Doing justly makes for more healthy communities. Political scientists teach us that opening the franchise to all without obstruction or violence leads to better politicians and better policies. Economists teach us that living wages, universal health care, dignified retirements, and progressive taxation improve quality of life for all of us. Theologians and preachers have shared that what we do *for* the least among us we do *for* G-d and what we do *to* the least among us we do *to* G-d. Psychologists warn us of the multiple traumas our refusal to be human inflicts upon so many.

Something is happening beyond the realm of intellect and reason. While it seems easy enough to address many of the problems I have named and the many I have not, there is a legacy of forces arrayed against what is right. These forces are entrenched. They are powerful and they do not yield without fierce fighting and struggle. These forces are inextricably linked in the deepest places of our memories and spirits. They are generationally embedded within us and around us. Often, we cannot tell where these forces end and where we begin. The battle before us will take place on the contested grounds of story and identity. And key players in the skirmishes ahead have been dead for decades if not centuries. They are our ancestors. They live at the water's edge. Ancestors of light aid us in safe passage. Shadow ancestors want us submerged in watery graves.

We live in a culture of ancestral worship and ancestral denial.

* * *

I remember when my parents purchased World Book encyclopedias for us in 1986. When these volumes arrived at our Jacksonville, Florida, home, I was filled with excitement. They were handsomely bound in burgundy leatherette with gold-leaf pages. They were prominently displayed in our home. Owning encyclopedias was a mark of the middle-class Black family and a declaration of commitment to education and worldliness.

I remember exactly where I began searching in those volumes almost forty years ago. I went looking for myself. I went looking for my people. I went looking for my ancestors. I still do not know exactly why I was so pressed to do this. The best I can come up with is that even as a twelve-year-old Black boy from Macon, Georgia, living in Jacksonville, Florida, I felt my very identity both underappreciated and under attack.

My home was filled with love and affirmation. My family and village supported and cheered me. But we all knew what America was, what Georgia was, what Florida was. We all knew that what my father said to us was true on multiple levels: "Those outside of this house do not love you like we do." This statement did not elicit fear but grounded me in reality. I could not live my entire life protected by the space Daddy and Momma lovingly created for my siblings and me. I needed to be aware of who I was and where I was at all times.

The pressures of being in a majority white neighborhood and school for the first time in my short life made me hyper aware of physical and spiritual realities inhospitable to my presence. I could not have articulated this at the time, but I needed shoring up and the World Book Encyclopedia came to my rescue. I looked up every African people group and every African nation. I looked up every Black woman and Black man. I turned each golden page searching for faces like mine. I was searching for my ancestors. I was looking for help to get through. I was searching for strength to jump in the water. I wanted to assert my identity in a hostile environment veneered with hospitality, as the South is wont to do.

The World Book Encyclopedia was no liberative publication. Its perspective on African cultures was rooted in an imperial, white gaze. But I consumed it all the same. I remember the encyclopedia would break down the population, languages, economic productivity, and religions of African nations. The writers of the entries dismissively called the majority of African people ancestor worshipers and animists. I remember that clearly in juxtaposition to the United States and European nations being called majority Christian.

I can now name what I felt then. White Americans and Europeans are ancestor worshipers, too. They just worship different ancestors toward different ends. Every time we rode by the statue of Andrew Jackson in Jacksonville, I felt fury. Though no one told me who the city was named after, as I recall, they didn't have to. I felt it.

How could a man so vile and bloodthirsty be so honored? He was an enslaver and an ethnic cleanser. Attaching his name and his image also attached his spirit to that place. Jacksonville is a case study of those challenges that make life burdensome for Black people and others. I lived, pastored, and organized there. The opposition to justice was fierce and those accepting of the city as it was, were many. Those asking questions—those asking why—seemed to be few. They were Black and they were white. And they would not trouble the water.

It's appropriate that in the Jacksonville statue, he's on horseback. Black churches sing a song entitled "Ride on, King Jesus." So with Jesus, so with Jackson. For white Jacksonians, he rides on through Florida in politics that strangle Black voters, purge the teaching of history, and endeavor to drive our LGBTQIA+ siblings underground. These policies are motivated by more than greed and racism and demographic anxiety. They are driven by ancestral commitments that survive and shape our current discourse. Those who named cities and counties after Andrew Jackson knew what they were doing. They were not only celebrating the man but also normalizing his brutality and cleansing the blood from his hands and garments. They chose not to name the land after a person who had been committed to the flourishing of all people. They named the land after a man committed to white supremacy. The political and spiritual realities of that decision are forever linked. Naming the spaces where humans live, love, laugh, and play after men like Andrew Jackson is an attempt to keep us on the high diving board. It is a strategy to normalize evil, misanthropic behavior. But many still wade in the water. And others jump. They make the waters roil.

Jackson was still galloping across Florida's panhandle in the late 1980s. When we moved to Tallahassee in 1988, I ran into him again. This time via a Tallahassee tradition called "Springtime Tallahassee." It was a celebration of Southern culture and territorial, antebellum Florida, complete with floats of Southern belles in hoop skirts and other nods to the "gallant South" and Lost Cause mythology. Springtime Tallahassee spoke loudest in what it never said and what it refused to remember, the way it scrubbed clean Indigenous removal, enslavement, and the hanging tree near Florida's Capitol. My homeboys and I were livid about Springtime Tallahassee's sanitized history designed to boost business and create the veneer of a kinder, gentler community minus the facts of history.

We protested. We spoke up in our high school classes. We refused to participate. And still Andrew Jackson rides on.

Those who invoked the spirits of Andrew Jackson and men of his ilk did so out of a sense of power and a belief that their status was secured by G-d, good breeding, and the ancestral power and blessing they craved. They may not have spoken of the spiritual power of their forebears. It would have been considered primitive, in poor taste, and possibly heretical. Yet, they built statues, monuments, and mythologies, and named cities, counties, and states after the dead whose legacies they extolled and extended. What was once done quietly and consistently from a place of power is now done forcefully and loudly out of a fear of impending impotence.

The rattling of white supremacist ancestral bones has intensified. Those who call the names of Jackson and Robert E. Lee and Jefferson Davis now do so out of grievance, fear, and a stubborn commitment to keep things as they were. They want us quiet and complacent. Shivering with fear at the water's edge.

Replacement theorists rattle ancestral bones. Republican politicians seeking to win primaries rattle ancestral bones. Right-wing media rattle ancestral bones. They may not call it such, but they know saying certain names, elevating images, and hoisting symbols gives them a surge of power. And every time they lift these names, images, and symbols, the shadow side of what Jesus said in the gospel of John comes to pass, and they draw all the angry, aggrieved, and afraid unto themselves.

* * *

Those who deny ancestral power deny humanity's fundamental need for story and purpose. The need to know that we do not travel alone. At age twelve I called upon ancestral power so that I could survive and thrive as a Black boy in a white world. My mother called on ancestral power, pushing me off the board and into the deep waters. Others called upon shadow ancestral power in Charlottesville, Virginia, in 2017 and at the Capitol on January 6, 2021, so that they could maintain white dominance at all costs.

We are all calling on ancestors. Some call for assistance as we pray for safe passage across turbulent waters. Others call for shadow forces to drown the bodies and souls of those who refuse this established order of death.

* * *

My first pastorate in Monticello, Florida, gave me a wonderful introduction to the vocation to which I've given my life. I served a family church where five generations worshiped together. The people of Saint Phillip taught me how to be a pastor. I am still drawing from the deep wells of ancestral wisdom I discovered there.

One day a relative of my congregants gave me a gift. It was a newly released biography of Florida freedom fighter

Harry T. Moore. I was thankful. I love books. But I wondered, *Why this book? Who is this man*? I tried to figure it out. This person had heard me preach. She had seen me in the community. We knew one another, but not well. I was moved by her generosity. I can see her now: a short, pistol of a woman. She talked fast and smiled easily. In the inscription, she basically said she wanted Harry T. Moore's story to intersect with my own. She thought we needed to know one another.

Mr. Moore's impact was so significant that none other than the great Langston Hughes memorialized him in a poem called "Ballad of Harry Moore." Mr. Moore was an educator, civil rights pioneer, and president of Florida's NAACP. He investigated lynchings, fought white-only primaries, demanded equal pay for Black teachers and significantly increased the Black vote in Florida. On the night of his twenty-fifth wedding anniversary a bomb exploded underneath his home. It was Christmas evening 1951. Harry Moore and his wife Harriette later died from injuries sustained during that vicious attack.

Previously Mr. Moore had been fired from his teaching job for demanding better pay for his Black colleagues. He had suffered economically because of his pursuit of justice. He and his wife gave all they had in service of human dignity and freedom.

Mr. Moore did not play a zero-sum game. It was not I win you lose. He was motivated by abundance. He risked his life on the proposition that there was enough freedom for us all. That none of us needs to lose. We can flourish together. Mr. Moore dove from the high board into the deep end.

Harry T. Moore is a cherished ancestor. The dear woman who introduced me to him has now herself ascended to the ancestral realm. I will never fully know her reasons, but I am thankful that she acquainted me with this man. And I know he is among the saints who share mystic communion with us. He is among the great cloud of witnesses cheering us to give our all in service of G-d's dream of creation flourishing together.

Andrew Jackson and Harry T. Moore both ride in Florida. And those who believe in freedom and liberation cannot embrace both ancestors. We must choose. Many make excuses for Andrew Jackson. They say he was a man of his time. They say we must not read his story according to our mores and values. But Andrew Jackson and those with him chose to take land by force and to extract the residents of that land through violence. Andrew Jackson and many of his time, whether occasional accounts show them being "polite" to the enslaved or not, chose to force people to labor to benefit others instead of paying fair wages for domestic and agricultural work. These choices are morally abhorrent. Human beings knew that then. Human beings know that now.

Harry T. Moore was also a man of his time. He could have chosen violence, but he did not. He could have chosen to accept Florida's violent racial apartheid. He did not. He questioned the system. He organized. He dove in. He won victories for the people, and he sustained defeat. Why does America excuse Jackson because he carried the banner for American imperialism while allowing Harry T. Moore to wax in anonymity? Which ancestor embodies the values we trumpet?

The ancestor Andrew Jackson cheers on our wars of aggression to expand territory, influence, and American business interests. The ancestor Harry T. Moore does not. Andrew Jackson will never stand against wage theft. Harry T. Moore will. It must never be lost on us that Donald Trump chose to hang a portrait of Jackson in a place of prominence in his White House.

We will never supersede the moral imaginations of the ancestors we venerate.

What can people tell about your ancestors by looking at the portraits on your wall or the books on your shelf? Whose portraits have you taken down? Whose portraits will you take down if you value liberation and community? And what price might you pay for letting go of ancestors your family, friends, and community venerate? If you are willing to pay that price, the ancestors we chose who have paid that price before are holding out their life-supporting hands. They have faced the waters. They go with you.

Our collective story is still being written. We can always change course. But we must choose to ride with the ancestors. With Harry T. Moore or with Andrew Jackson? The decision we make is the foundation upon which our collective identity will be built.

* * *

Genesis 3 records that G-d took a walk in the garden. I have always felt this text deeply in my bones. I hear G-d's footsteps pushing up fresh earth in the infant garden. I feel the breeze generated by divine motion. I hear G-d breathing in frustration as G-d searches for us, the crown jewel of creation, bone of G-d's bone and flesh of G-d's flesh.

We were hiding. Concocting a story of our own, independent of our creator. And G-d came looking for us. Could anything else have aroused G-d to leave the place where G-d dwells to come to our realm? We had turned the garden into a place of scarcity. We ignored the abundance dancing before us. We zeroed in on one fruit among millions. We wanted the fruit that would help us to declare independence from G-d and one another. Though it tastes of death, this is still our favorite fruit.

We bit and we hid. We covered our beautiful vulnerability in a futile attempt to lean fully into the lies we were told and were telling. And the first prayer happens in the form of a question. We do not pray to G-d. G-d prays to us. G-d asks, "Where are you?" I don't believe G-d ever stops asking this question.

Where are we in relation to G-d, the great Ancestor? Where are we in relation to each other? Where are we in relation to creation? G-d walks toward us in the beauty of what G-d has made and asks us the only question that matters: Where are you?

When we heard G-d coming our answer was fear. When we realized our vulnerability and utter dependence upon G-d and one another our answer was fear. Fear was our ancestral answer in the text. And for too many of us, fear remains our answer. This does not have to be.

What if we answered G-d, saying "G-d, we want to follow you out of this story we are telling ourselves. We want to walk out of here clothed in the vulnerability we knew before we declared our independence." Maybe the story would have ended differently.

Where are we? There are ancestors who can show us the way. There are ancestors who do not hide when G-d comes near. In fear and faith, they walk toward G-d, and they can teach us to do the same.

We must let go of ancestors whose lives and ongoing energy are rooted in fear. A commitment to the politics of scarcity and a hubris rooted in a refusal to accept the role of the created, not the creator, led many who came before us to rob, steal, kill, exploit, and enslave. I am not interested in excavating the personal indiscretions of the dead. I *am* interested in the theological, political, economic, and social systems that ancestors built to accumulate power at all costs. These systems are demonic machines whose friction is lubricated by human blood, sweat, and tears. The living and the dead conspire to keep these machines running efficiently the world over. In this moment we are called to shut down these systems of death once and for all.

I have marveled at the power of injustice and evil to flourish. Our academic ancestors have offered us alternatives and we have refused them. Our ancestor preachers have sought to inspire us rhetorically and theologically toward embracing the ethics of peace and shared prosperity. We looked away. Our artist ancestors sang, wrote, danced, and painted us into new worlds. If we take up residence in that beauty, most of us refuse to stay for very long.

The ancients knew that the dead remain with us. We sense it too, but our epistemological arrogance often keeps us from embracing the wisdom of the ages. They ride on, leading us to life or death. Their ideas have not died. Their systems have not died. The light they left behind remains. And their shadows remain.

Every morning I wake up believing that the world as it is, is not the world G-d intended. I believe the world can be changed. I marshal every resource at my disposal in my quest to leave the world better than I found it. I have joined communities committed to justice. I have read books by sacred ancestors and attended lectures by the present witnesses to justice. I have prayed, preached, and organized. But there is another power. It is like the wind, invisible to the eye, but when aroused capable of rearranging everything we see. Our ancestors are that wind. And all of us have felt it.

The divine is hovering in the wind and the divine will meet us in the waters. The waters around us are turbulent, but we don't have to be afraid to jump in. We are not alone. My mother pushed me in. I am so glad that she did. Yes, the misanthropic politics of Andrew Jackson are still in the waters, but Harry T. Moore taught me how to outmaneuver the waves of Jacksonian violence and to calm the waters for refuge and justice in their wake. As we navigate the waters, we must remain curious and communally focused, knowing we meet and care for humanity in these raging seas. Not all of us will survive, but G-d's dream for the world and our commitment to the waters of justice will never die! Jump!

2

Ancestral Awakenings

I RECALL A jazz concert in the early 1990s in Tucker Hall's Charles Winter Wood Theater on the highest of seven hills in Tallahassee, Florida. Nat Adderley was the featured artist. Actually, the featured artist *is* Nat Adderley. He plays on.

As I listened to him play, I sensed his father, Julian Carlyle, and his brother Julian Edwin, known as "Cannonball," trading buoyant licks with him from beyond the veil. These artists had taught and learned and played at my alma mater. They had walked the hills that all Rattlers walk. And now, they rest.

But no one told their music they were gone. On that night, thirty years ago, they played through and with Nat. There was no question. Nat wove narrative and song into a death-defying, time-bending thing. I don't know the words to describe it. Even the word *concert* is way too pedestrian.

I never wanted the music to stop playing. It was delicious. A feast for ear, eye, heart, and spirit. I heard the conversation between musical partners—sometimes complimenting one another, sometimes complaining about one another, always climbing higher. I saw salty sweat glistening from foreheads and flung from flying fingers. I saw bodies swaying as they gave birth to notes and silence.

I felt like I was traveling. Like a conductor had punched my ticket. The forward motion across the terrain of self was undeniable. Sometimes fast. Sometimes slow. The music was talking to me at levels deeper than rationality. It was ushering me forward. It was chastising me. I could not make out every word. It was like being in the next room when adults are talking as a child. You can't make out every word, but you desperately want to. But you know, intuit, something is happening, you get the sense of it. And even when you do hear complete sentences, most of it goes right over your head.

Ancestors are musicians. And the music is always playing. Always. When we cannot hear it is not because there is no music. It is because we have not received ears to hear. Hearing requires desire on our part and on the part of ancestors. They must want us to hear. We must want to hear more than we don't want to hear.

Sometimes I want to hear. Other times I don't.

* * *

In the landscape where I live and move, it can seem that there are also other ancestors who are most loquacious and the ones I least want to hear. Theirs is the macabre music of conquest and death. They are the ancestors of monuments that abound to memorialize them in Washington, DC, and elsewhere. They are warriors and scions of wealth and industrial power. These ancestors seized people and places. Their names adorn buildings and are wed to scholarships that create shiny, young neoliberals who continue their global regime. Some think they are dead and buried. To me, neither is true.

On a chilly December day in 2020, I stood outside of Metropolitan African Methodist Episcopal Church in Washington, DC. The wind laughed at my attempt to bundle up to withstand its lashes. Despite the weather I committed to stand watch with our security team in front of our church as scores of Trump supporters walked past our storied house of worship. Some quieted down when they walked past an unquestionably Black church. Some got louder so that we could overhear their conversations. A few hurled epithets our way. They vocalized their disapproval that we occupied space so close to the holiest site of their Trumpian faith. To them our presence was pollution. It fouled their field of vision. The fragrance of our rootedness in that place, which we have occupied since the 1880s, was olfactorily abhorrent to them. We had no business being blocks from the White House.

They were not walking alone. An innumerable ancestral caravan traveled with them. Inspiring, literally breathing into, their speech and action. They were defiant and convinced of the rightness of their anti-Blackness and their power to lay claim to our land and, if necessary, to lay siege to us.

Not many days after this, the Proud Boys breached our property. They crossed Metropolitan's M Street Northwest–facing iron gate on a Saturday night to worship their ancestors, to extol their gods. Their call to worship was familiar. They claimed the deity as their own and divinity as their exclusive birthright. Their scriptures were taken from books of racist pseudoscience and white domination. There was no offertory. They gave nothing save to take everything. What intrigues me beyond their threadbare texts and sociopathic sermons is their hymnody. What songs do people sing who feel they have the power to own, to take, to destroy? What is their music? What of their soundtrack?

After this happened, I was asked repeatedly how I felt, how we felt, after the events of this ancestor worship. Was I angry? Anger is an emotion tied to emotional investment. I value the humanity even of domestic terrorists. But I expect them to not violate our holy places. So, I was not angry. Was I sad? No. Sadness implies that those who perpetrated this act could conversely have made me happy. They have no such power. I was resigned. I was focused. I was leaning into ancestral spaces that were steeling me, soothing me with music.

These "Black and unknown bards of long ago," as James Weldon Johnson called them, indeed had lips that had touched the sacred fire. With singed lips, and blazing hearts, and radiant minds they composed music that has moved me, that has moved our human family to higher heights and deeper depths. I heard one such song in the literal and figurative sanctuaries of my youth—"Up above my head / I hear music in the air / There must be a God somewhere."

This song is confession and manifesto. The singer is both convinced and in need of convincing. Above my head, beyond what can be fully known at present, beyond what the senses can easily recognize, something or someone beckons me. The ground beneath me is real. I feel it. It contains mysteries I know, like planting and harvesting, burying, and trusting the power of new life. And there are mysteries the ground beneath me has yet to reveal. I live in that tension between revelation and mystery.

I see the world in front of me and behind me. I know the love and laughter it offers. I experience the joy of human connection and nature's manifold gifts. But I also know brutality and cruelty and exploitation. This plane's possibilities thrill me. And its countless broken promises, which taste of blood and smell like decomposing dreams, envelop and choke me.

I live the things beneath me. But I do not sing them. I live the things before me and behind me. But I do not sing them. I sing of what is above my head. I believe that someone, that something, above my head can transform that which is beneath me, before me, and behind me.

Above my head I hear music permeating the air. The music plays. It plays for me as I write. It plays for you as you read. Do you want to hear it? It is delightful music. Never have you heard sounds so compelling and captivating. The music will draw you and pull you in the direction of freedom. And freedom is dangerous in the American empire. Free people will not be controlled; thus, the religious, economic, and political systems that vivify empire will do all they can to shackle and to chain you. Be warned. For the shackled and the chained, the music grows ever louder. For them there is but one song, "Get free!"

Do you want to hear it? It is the music of awareness. It will never allow you to live comfortably in the status quo again. It will not let you pretend not to see what you see. You will no longer be able to pretend that you do not hear what you hear. You will see our ancestor Toni Cade Bambara. She will sing the song that can make us new, "What are we pretending not to know today?" This song arrests feigned ignorance and frees prisoners trapped behind bars of self-imposed unawareness.

Is it possible to hear this music? Can we sing this song? Only if we dance between awareness and delight.

The music is not exclusively available to the singer. It is available to all. But the music cannot be owned or commodified. It defies the allure of venture capital. It does not create private property or individual wealth. This music nourishes the one who values community and indicts the progeny of Narcissus.

Even, maybe especially, those who sing this song find themselves wrestling with the existence of the Divine. "Up above my head / I hear music in the air / there must be a God somewhere." Manifesto. I hear music. I am committed. I will run to see what the end will be. These ancestors remind us that confession is sprinkled with doubt—there *must* be a G-d somewhere; not there *is* a G-d somewhere. I hear struggle. I do not hear weak resignation to imposed dogma or inherited religious sensibilities. I hear the singer belting out, "I want to believe! Make me believe! Show me something!"

In wisdom, the singer connects the music to the possible existence of G-d. The singer is sure of the existence of the music. She hears it. And there is hope that the music will lead to the Mystery beyond mystery.

Are the ancestors calling? Have you stilled yourself long enough to hear the sounds above your head? Do you, like me, often fill your days with sounds, with streaming shows, with podcasts, and with mindless chatter in a feeble attempt to make the music go away? It won't.

It demands to be heard. It is an inner music that guides and directs. You can no more stop the music than you can stop the sun from rising or waves from crashing upon the shore. We keep watch for the music like we await the sun's appearance each morning. Listen for the music like you listen for waves at the beach. Part of delighting in sunrise is our awareness that the golden orb appears without our aid. The marvel of the incessant music of crashing waves is that no human stands on the beach with a baton coaxing melodies from the ocean. We marvel partly because we are acknowledging our lack of control. At this ancient, ancestral music we can learn to marvel. This music is as real and uncontrollable as sun and surf.

Ancestors offer us powerful rhythms that do joyful battle with songs and singers whose music dehumanizes and causes despair. Be nourished by these songs, these spirituals, these psalms of life, hope, and resistance set to sublime melodies and piercing silences.

My ancestors gave me music with so much more. My paternal grandmother and my aunt gave me music that reoriented my politics and theology. This music did not come from a hymnal, it came from a . . . mall. And I have yet to reckon fully with this music's holiness, its otherness. This music was both immanent and transcendent, filled with the Source of all things and the myriad complexities that make us human.

My paternal grandmother's name was Sallie. We called her Mommee. She was loving and generous. She lavished sugary treats upon us. We ate many a square pizza, many a sweet potato pie, and many a biscuit made by her loving hands. We watched soap operas, also known as "the stories," with her. We watched her beloved Atlanta Braves on TBS. I loved to see her fall asleep by the seventh inning. We had sapped her afternoon strength after she had returned home from a hard day's work. Don't be fooled though. She was also stern and in the parlance of Black folk in the South, she didn't play the radio. She didn't even own a radio!

Her daughter, my father's sister, was Juanita. As is the custom of many who share my culture, we called her Sister. Her friends called her LaLa. She personified style and cool. She was committed to her family and was a source of constant laughter and encouragement in the lives of her nieces and nephews. When she came home, we all lit up like Christmas trees. And during yuletide season even more: she gave us cash. Best. Gift. Ever.

I would count my money. Arrange it by denominations. Smell it. Smooth it out. And constantly check to make sure it had not disappeared into the ether. My mother was right. That money was burning a hole in my pocket. I could not wait to spend it.

During the Christmas season of 1985, I only wanted one thing. I wanted music. I got a double-cassette stereo with a turntable on top. We had a floor model Curtis Mathes television with an AM/FM stereo, 8-track player, and a turntable. But I did not believe in communal ownership. I wanted my own!

I knew the joy of my father's cassette tapes and records. But that was no longer good enough for me. I was smelling myself. The money that burned my pockets was destined for the record store in the Macon Mall.

On the day after Christmas, Mommee and Sister drove us to the mall to buy what we wanted with our Christmas stashes. We lined up for the modern liturgy of frantic spending in the temple of commerce and we were as happy as we could be. I wanted only one thing. One record. I went to the bin and selected it. I showed it to them for their approval as the adults with charge over us. I am sure they had no clue what the music was. Maybe they trusted me. Maybe they knew I would find a way to get it even if they disapproved. Maybe they knew that any kid that wanted music this bad should not be stopped. It was *an* LP. It was *the* LP. LL Cool J's *Radio*.

I don't know where that record is now. It doesn't matter. Every word is lodged in my head. LL Cool J wasn't the first hip-hop artist I was aware of. But his image captured my imagination. He was me. Black and young. He wasn't me. Muscular and cool. He was me. A lover of words and rhythm. He wasn't me. An urbane New Yorker with a record deal. I was a corny, bespectacled kid in love with a style of music that was New York, but it was also Georgia. It was as much James Brown as it was James Todd Smith. I felt it.

I was eleven years old, connecting Daddy's Isaac Hayes 8-tracks and Marvin Gaye records to the sights and sounds of my generation. It wasn't new stuff so much as it was water from the same rich, Black rivers flowing through the contours of my generation. This music was and is a complex gift from the ancestors. It helped me to hear their voices anew demanding that I be bold and loud like my radio while remembering as Cool J taught us, "I Need Love."

That music came to me, to us, in the middle of the Reagan era's Hollywood-inflected boosterism of states' rights (death for Black people), militarism (death for Black and poor people the world over), and the glories of casino capitalism, neoliberalism, and the Chicago School's economics (slow death for humans and the planet). Reagan's rhetoric gave a smiling, strident voice to American ancestral calls to demonize the poor, ignore the suffering (especially of those with HIV/AIDS), whittle away Black citizenship gains and voting rights—all while signing legislation that made Martin Luther King Jr.'s birthday a federal holiday.

I grooved when I listened to Cool J like I grooved when I listened to Daddy's 45s of James Brown's "The Big Payback" and "Mother Popcorn." The music purchased that day connected with the music already in me. And the music Cool J created was of a piece with the music in him. Maybe that's what Mommee and Sister knew. I am sure they thought, "Billy has his own music." It was a contemporary iteration of the beats and rhythms that make surviving both sweet and possible.

Radio had a big radio on the front cover. That was the symbol of vim and vigor for young Black men in the eighties. Those loud boxes disturbed many, but they were a declaration. We are here! We will be heard! I am not invisible! You will hear me! You will hear us! Plus, the music, it was just so good.

My grandmother and aunt are the ancestors who connected me to the music that opened doors for me intellectually, politically, and theologically. LL led to Run DMC and Run DMC led to Public Enemy and Public Enemy led to Boogie Down Productions. They refused to keep me from the tangible expressions of the music of my generation—records. My room was filled with these records and images and sounds that were challenging me. I had never questioned what the church taught me until I listened to Chuck D and KRS-One. I had never heard of John Coltrane or Joanne Deborah Chesimard or Louis Farrakhan or Steve Biko. This music stirred up the music inside of me. This music connected me with ancestors and contemporaries who welcomed me when I learned of them and summoned them. And all of this was facilitated by my ancestors—Mommee and Sister.

But the ancestors' wisdom taught me that ancestors do not want us to mimic their music. They want us to know the sounds of their music so that we can reverently and beautifully play our own music, nourished by the blessed fountain of memory. To summon the ancestral is not a call for us to be ossified, calcified, and fossilized around nostalgic notions. Ancestral rhythms grace us to detect the footprints of our mothers and fathers.

We will know where to walk and we will know where not to walk because of danger they have already discovered. When we no longer detect footprints, we will fly with them. Those are the places where the winds of new worlds are blowing, and the ground can no longer hold the majesty that is us.

I cannot recall how deeply Mommee and Sister scrutinized LL's first album, which was also mine, before they allowed me to glide giddily to the cashier. They could have directed me toward a more practical purchase. They could have judged it or called it devil's music. They could have forecast that the doom of Billy would commence when he placed the needle into the groove of this strange record. But they trusted me. Mommee and Sister trusted me. There is no way I would have been able to purchase the album without their consent. I did not grow up in a democracy. They let me decide. They trusted me to become.

Ancestors have a stake in our becoming new.

The faith that I inherited is *ancestor* drenched even as the word was not used frequently. But what does the Apostles' Creed mean when it affirms that we believe in the communion of saints? Our faith is nurtured and nourished by those who came before us. Death does not erase them. They linger. They commune with us. Share space with us. Love us. Laugh with us. Laugh at us. Rejoice with us. Mourn with us. They made the music that is the soundtrack of our lives.

Consider this: All that we do is either expanded or contracted by those who thought and lived before us. How we think about theology, economics, and politics is circumscribed or widened by ancestors. The tunes they played have not ceased to dictate the movements of the human dance.

From my youngest days this mystery has gripped me. Stories of my ancestors did not just strike me as words and memories. Those stories conjured ancestors. They called ancestors forth and made them materialize before me. I craved those stories because they gave me substance and density. Those stories are creating me still.

* * *

I remember a strange day. My cousin Tina and I were lying on the floor at Nanny's house. CBS's soap opera lineup from the 1980s provided ambient sound and visuals. We were telling each other stories that we had heard about our deceased relatives. Tina was about eight years old. I was all of six. We did this for a long time. Where had we heard these stories? Who told us? As reflected some four decades later, those stories had become part of our very bodies. Narrative had become blood and marrow. Each fragment of each story was not just heard, it was chewed and swallowed and flowed through us.

We heard them say how tall Big Daddy was. How thin he was. That he had fought in World War I. That he was the leader of the Brothers and Sisters of Love Mutual Aid Society of Jones County, Georgia. He had a typewriter and a telephone and a vision for his family. Even as Tina and I spoke those words my life was taking shape within them. And before he died, he sent his granddaughters out of the room because G-d had told him his time had come.

We heard them say that Grandpa Arthur had a beautiful tenor voice and sang Langston Hughes's *Black Nativity*. We knew that he sold Atlanta Life Insurance, and that he was a deacon at First Baptist Church. He kept his head bald with the same clippers my daddy used to shave when I was a boy. He purchased burial plots for his family and bought a brand-new car with credit life insurance. He knew his time was coming. And he died one room over from where Tina and I lay side by side, talking about him.

I had met Big Daddy, but he died a mere eight months after my birth. And Grandpa Arthur died before we could ever hear his voice or see his smile. We had no living memories of Big Daddy or Grandpa Arthur, but we had *all* the memories. And on that strange day Tina and I wept. On that strange day, Tina and I physically grieved our ancestors. Our bodies had taken on the joy of the presence of these ancestors. And now our bodies expressed and released the pain associated with their physical absence.

What kind of children do this? Children who hear and feel and know because they listen to the ancestors speaking. Many children, of varying ages, need to listen, to share the stories, to lie down and weep and grieve for ancestors in our day. Tina and I knew Presence. And we knew presence.

* * *

Music fills the air. The Divine is the conductor. We are the voices. We are the instruments. As I reflect on the soulful, sweaty, sublime music of Nat Adderley, the music that opened this chapter and the music chapters of my life, I am aware that Nat and those who played with him opened themselves for the Divine music to play through them. And Nat's father and brother were embodied in that Divine music. Even after they died, Nat never played without them.

In the music of ancestors, dear reader, there are no soloists. Ancestral music originates in Source. It originates "above our heads." When you sing, you are not singing alone. Singing in and through you is the Ancient of Days. Singing in and through you are ancestors, by blood and bond, who have chosen you to push forward the work that will never be complete in a lifetime.

I have been surrounded by those who connected me to the music of freedom. And ancestors are waiting to connect you to this same freedom music. Some of these ancestors you and I share. Some are ones my family, and my community, knows. My ancestors are those whom I knew as elders when I was younger. They no longer live, but they are *alive.* Then I met ancestors in music. They danced off records and tapes and CDs and into my essence. I met ancestors in books and documentaries. I met them in stories and lectures. They called to me because they lived lives defined by love and liberation. I am singing my way into answering yes when they call me to be who I am called to be and to do what I am called to do.

The music I have mentioned is a symphony that brings us together as those made in the image and likeness of G-d. We are human. We are divine. We can cocreate a world different than this one. The spark of the eternal rests in us and upon us.

There is other ancestor music. It is cacophonous. Tina and I wept because we could feel the weight of death all around us. We heard and felt death's music and our little bodies and spirits responded. We did not know the limits of death. We only knew death punched hard. And knew the ancestors who lived the wisdom of freedom. Both of those ancestors we met that day, with "the stories" on TV and the stories that took form in us, as we listened, and as the ancestors spoke.

3

Naming Our Ancestors

AN ANCESTOR IS one who is no longer physically present, but whose energy, radiance, and shadow continue to pierce our reality in life-giving—or death-dealing—ways. Ancestors are not just those from whom we may be directly descended. And ancestors are not just those to whom we may be related by blood.

Ancestors, like living humans, contain the spark of the divine. They are beings beyond our creation and control. From African cultures I have learned of the sublime notion of G-d as the great and primary ancestor, something James Weldon Johnson's poetic vision "The Creation" explores. A maternal and paternal Being, the one who created us all, G-d also desires fellowship with humans. Our ancestors, those radiant and those shadowy, also find their origin in this One.

When we call our ancestors' names, we are not merely speaking. By calling their names we are reinscribing limits or transgressing boundaries. We are arousing death or summoning life. When we tell our ancestors' stories we are rediscovering and traveling upon well-worn paths as well as escorting younger generations, for good or for ill, along with us.

My iteration of the Black church is skeptical of even the word *ancestor*. Many of the keepers of my tradition seem to believe that there is something heterodox about naming ancestors. Those who name ancestors are considered to be tangoing with apostasy. The mere mention of ancestors is thought to supplant the primacy of G-d or Jesus or the Holy Spirit. There is real tension here, taut as can be.

However, there is no faith without naming ancestors. The names of many of our holy books honor ancestors. Matthew, Mark, Luke, John, Isaiah, Jeremiah, Ezekiel. These books call forth ancestral remembrance, though we may be too far removed to name it as such. Many of the writers of these texts wrote pseudepigraphically—in the name of revered ancestors—so that their words or anthologies would get a hearing. Historically, when associating with those of significance, as with biblical texts, that made, and still makes, contemporary hearing possible.

And prayer. The saints of the church would begin their prayers by wedding G-d to the ancestors and the ancestors to G-d. Countless times I've heard committed churchmen and churchwomen chanting this divine appellation in the context of worship: "God of Abraham, God of Isaac, God of Jacob, have mercy upon us!" These prayers interweave the divine and the ancestral rhetorically and theologically. Ancestors are not claimed to be Source, but ancestors illumine Source and name Source. This is no slippery slope toward the theological abyss, but a show of the thin line connecting the human and the divine. The Creator is named by and with Creation. As such, ancestral speech becomes divine speech, and divine speech becomes ancestral speech. There appears to be no way to locate G-d apart from ancestors. The divine cannot be saved from the oily smudge of human fingerprints. Our G-d-talk is always human and ancestral. And locating G-d among any people group is always an ancestral act. As is seeing G-d at work among a people: It's impossible to do without naming those who came before.

Black church as I experienced it was always an ancestral recitation. Miriam. Moses. Bathsheba. David. Lydia. Paul. G-d's story was told through their stories. G-d's life was mediated through human foibles and achievements. We cannot square my tradition's fear of ancestors with its practice. In reality, the Black church is ancestor drenched even as it clings to something akin to ancestor phobia. What is this? Why is this? On display is a policing of the ancestors. More on this later, but at its root, the truth is some are welcome. Others are not.

When the world is alive with ancestors statues of them, cemeteries filled with their bones, buildings named for them, books written by them, images of them—why do we so often hide from their reality, their influence? Black churches are filled with pictures and portraits of the faithful departed. Pews and Sunday school rooms are named for those who have fallen asleep. Cornerstones are etched with ancestral names and church auxiliaries and ministries are developed and tagged with the names of the deceased, lest we forget. With all this ancestral energy swimming and singing and reverberating around us, why would we pretend that their grip on us is not palpable, sometimes even determinative?

We must interrogate our feigned ancestral avoidance. Do we just name people, places, and things after the dead because we have nothing better to do? Or is there something innate within us that guides us in ancestral directions?

Why, in my home state of Georgia, are innumerable counties, cities, villages, and hamlets named after Confederates? And why have Black people in the same state named their high schools and community centers and social clubs after Phillis Wheatley, Booker T. Washington, George Washington Carver, and Mary McLeod Bethune? Is this naming about more than preserving memory? It seems we want the very places where we live and work to carry the sacred energy of our forebears.

We may not use the word *ancestor*. We may be uncomfortable with the power the word conjures. We may even think that we avoid ancestral realities altogether. But our very lives, and the very places where we live and move and have our being, testify against us. We can no more avoid ancestors as avoid ourselves.

The Booker T. Washington Community Center was a source of life and pride in the Pleasant Hill Community of Macon, Georgia. I remember seeing beautiful Black people going into the center to meet, to play, and to pray. We went to the center to augment our lack of groceries and to flourish in an abundance of Black joy. I suspect we had to fight to get the city to fund our recreation place. The last thing the white power structure of Macon was interested in was Black people recreating anything, especially the social order that did its best to extract from us and to crush us. Our dogged determination to create something new and beautiful in the name of one who had gone before meant they were unsuccessful at ridding themselves of us.

The Black elders who nourished me, ancestors now, over-invested in the young. And the investment was ancestral and forward looking. They named the center after the Wizard of Tuskegee. And when we excelled in Sunday school, when we recited the memory verse flawlessly, when we won the district declamation contests, they rewarded us with Booker T. Washington half dollars. And even when we didn't win, come Christmas, we got Booker T. Washington half dollars because we were theirs and they were ours. Because they knew us to be beautiful and desired nothing more than our flourishing, and Booker T. Washington was the name of both ancestry and future.

Someone, probably Mr. Persylvia R. Perry, a tall, dark man with glowing white hair, our Sunday school superintendent or his designee, would go to the bank and got these half dollars for each student. Yes, it would have been easier to just give the currency with which we were most familiar. But they were making a statement: This currency contains our image. Our achievement. Our possibility. Our pain. I am not sure how deeply they gave themselves over to meditations like this, but they were strategic in all they did and said concerning the younger generation. The names and images and gifts they gave were rooted in a thoughtfulness forged on the anvil of Black alchemy: We are masters of making sugar from shit.

My great-grandparents named their youngest son Booker T. Lamar. He is now the patriarch of our family. Saying his name stirs me. I wish I could ask Big Momma and Big Daddy why they named their manchild Booker T. in 1939. Was it because of their regard for the Wizard? Probably. Were they speaking excellence over their sixth son? Were they offering a map for him, for us? Of course, naming children after significant figures is nothing new. But it takes on a different meaning for those living within a culture that is intentionally hostile to your existence. It means something different for those living in a culture that makes a religion of destroying your bodies and trying desperately to strangle the oxygen from your soul.

My elders were busy living. My grandfather Henry Orlando Lamar Sr. had a chair. It was his chair. No one sat in it. We hadn't earned the privilege. I spent my undergraduate spring breaks driving from Tallahassee to Macon to spend time with my paternal grandfather and my maternal grandmother. To sit near the chairs where they sat, to hear their voices and to behold the beauty of their being, was pure joy for me. I said no to Freaknik and all manner of undergraduate shenanigans and chose to bask in the presence of my forebears. My 1984 Chevrolet Cavalier knew the way to their homes, which were my homes. I would spend half of spring break week with my grandfather and the other half with my grandmother. I knew that unless life took one of those tragic turns it's wont to do, I had more time than they had, and I was committed to squeezing every drop of sweet juice from the peach of their presence.

My grandfather watched the news all day long. It was CNN or C-SPAN. No sports. No silly sitcoms. If he was at home, he was knee deep in current affairs, geopolitical events, and politics. He read the world clearly and without sentiment. He knew when he was being gaslit. He knew when spin doctors had prepared speeches. And he knew when leaders were out of their depth. He kept himself immersed, watching, thinking, and serving and just being present until the age of 89. And he was no more.

Yet, I dreamed of him last night. Gone, but here. Even when diminished by the weight of nearly nine decades pressing upon him, his brain kept buzzing and his powers of observation never diminished. During one of those spring break visits he told me something that I will never forget. "Boy," he said, "I ain't gonna rust out. I'm gonna wear out." My grandfather and so many of his generation named their progeny *life* in a sea of American manufactured death.

Everything about him said, *live*. Said, *I am going to live until there is no more life left in me! And then I will live some more*! I saw them down. I saw them grieve. I have no idea what they harbored in the private counsels of their hearts. But I know they lived at great cost to themselves. They dwelled in and upon life. They were not distracted by white folk doing what white folk do. They were not distracted by America doing what America does. They lived and they gave us names that were markers of this stubborn commitment to life.

My mother's mother, Nanny, endured unspeakable violence. I will not write about it. But it is worse than you are imagining. I met Aunt Viney in her home. Nanny is largely responsible for my attempt to puzzle through the ancestral. What did Nanny name us? Nanny named us *beauty*. Her porch was filled with gorgeous, colorful flowers. She was committed to beauty. Her home was adorned by the flowers she arranged. She made every dress in my mother's wedding party. She made my cousin a wedding dress from plastic bread bags. She made beauty by teaching us to memorize the poetry she loved by James Weldon Johnson and Paul Laurence Dunbar. Nanny was beautiful and Nanny named us *beauty* in an ugly world.

Our ancestors named us to facilitate our thriving and not just our survival. They named us after people so that we would search them out and know that we are not alone and that we owe something to generations of old and generations to come. They also named us, by the environments they created, after virtues and values. They named us *beauty* and *faith* and *life* and *dignity*. They named and modeled. They loved and demanded. They cursed and prayed. Without brick or straw they built houses we still inhabit.

I live in houses built by my Black ancestors. I answer to the many names they gave me. Names that keep my joy alive.

Names that prepare me for the harsh realities that life visits upon us all. They whispered names over me that I have yet to hear. I am growing into these names, living into these names. This is salvation: I am still discovering my name.

I also live in houses named and built by white ancestors. The stubborn, unjust, and seemingly intractable political economy of the United States of America is a house in which I dwell. The architects of this house designed an edifice replete with trapdoors. Progress seems illusory and short-lived. The amendments and laws designed to give bondspersons their liberty were twisted and made to support corporate personhood, not Black personhood. Hard won voting rights were sacrificed in this century by ending Justice Department preclearance before states with histories of violent, bloody voter suppression could change their voting laws. The precarity of bodily autonomy for women was abandoned by the law as well. This house traps and tricks. It promises shelter but abandons many to the chaos of howling winds and driving rain. This house promises warmth while exposing the most vulnerable to the arctic chill of being left to struggle and flail in a house that refuses to be shelter, to be home.

Who designed this house? Ancestors. Long dead and very much alive. We cling to their systems: capitalism, racism, and imperialism. We cling as if there is no other way to order our lives together. We lament the outcome of the systems they left us. We hang our heads because we know these systems gorge themselves on human blood and treasure. We cry crocodile tears about what these systems produce. But we seem unwilling and unable to do the work of unraveling them in the interest of human flourishing.

The ancestors who built this American house named it *freedom*, *justice*, and *equality*. But these names are merely written on the walls. They are written in erasable marker, not in permanent ink. And what matters most is not what is written on the walls. The walls of houses are torn down and moved frequently, often thoughtlessly. What matters most is the foundation these ancestors created for the house. We must ask, of what material is this American house built? Is it watertight? Can it be washed away by torrents of truth?

In his poem "Let America Be America Again," Langston Hughes said that America was never America to him. We were not welcome. We were surveilled. Mistrusted. Questioned. Wings clipped. Flight inhibited. I feel that way in the contemporary American house. And I always feel the Ancestor shadow presence. These white ancestors stand guard still. They intend to keep this house as it is. They watch nervously when we spread our wings and then they do all they can to keep us from flying. This house is crumbling, and they refuse to rebuild the house, from the foundation up. There is still enough room in the house. There always has been. But they would rather collapse the house than accommodate us all.

Those in the American ancestral house, call me by many names. I do not answer. They want me to answer in gratitude. They believe I should exhibit gratitude for being in this house. I will not. They call me "exceptional." This is their trick to make me think that I am different or better than the *we*. I refuse to turn my head. There are millions like me. Does calling me exceptional allay their fear? They couldn't bear the knowledge of all the exceptional, ungrateful Black people I know and love. They call me "opportunity." They bid me look at all they have placed before me. I walk away.

I walk toward ancestors who know my name, who name my story and share theirs with mine.

The names of people, places, and things carry intent and values. So when names and stories are erased, they reveal a politics. Names and stories forgotten malform our world. Without knowing the names and stories and struggles and joys of those intentionally and strategically disappeared by the owners of this American house, we will continue to sit in a crumbling structure. Our fall is imminent.

That is why I walk on with those who know my name, who share their name, and who walk with me in the present and toward the future.

Don't you know that the erasure of human stories is violence? It is the worst kind of violence. Those who own this house, their ancestors who designed this house, think that they can kill humans in life and kill them again after they have died by burying their stories, their promise, their pain, their names. But science teaches that mass can neither be created nor destroyed. Not by crumbling houses, not by the toxic chemicals systematically splashed upon us to destroy our being and our stories. The mass that is our essence will never go into that good night. It lives on, fights on, and loves on in the ancestral energy that never ceases to call us to be more human and more aware of the divinity that enfolds us.

One of the hymns my people sang with vigor was "I Am on the Battlefield for My Lord." That song was ubiquitous. I heard G-d's sable children sing this song throughout the southeastern United States. Old Black women, hands gnarled by grueling work, sang it. Stooped Black men, struggling to stand erect, belted it. Little Black boys like me, surrounded by this divine, dark host in prayer meetings and in worship, knew every word. We sang with tears and with joy. Why did this hymn resonate so? Why did it travel to every hill and holler where Black folk set out to encounter the Ancient of Days? Why were we so happy to be on the battlefield? Isn't there significant risk? Won't there be casualties?

In those African Methodist Episcopal and Baptist churches, they understood deeply and richly that the Lord's battlefield was an inner reality and a historical, political reality. There was no bifurcation. There was no sacred-secular split. The world was the Lord's battlefield and fighting was not optional, but necessary. Fighting within to conquer that which seeks to conquer our souls. That is war. Fighting without, fighting every individual and system that would deny, desecrate, and denigrate. That is war. This song communicated a communal commitment to show up and to name a battle a battle. And to serve in the ranks until death. And then serve some more. That song was a spiritual and political awakening for me before I knew that I needed to be awakened. That song named me a soldier in the army of the Lord.

* * *

Not only have ancestors named me and you and the places where our feet trod. Our ancestors have named the Divine. The first person to name G-d in scripture is Hagar. She escapes the unspeakable violence of Abram and Sarai and names G-d *El Roi*, the One who sees. And even as ancestors like Hagar name G-d, G-d sees and names our ancestors. My forebears named G-d *Battle Axe*. Listen to the lyrics as interpreted by Deacon Ulysses Saffold and Rev. Dr. Arthur Timothy Jones:

> *He's a battle axe*
> *In the time of a battle . . .*
> *Shelter in the time of a storm*

White, liberal seminary professors told me that military metaphors should be avoided in the theological and homiletical enterprise. My mothers and fathers thought and sang differently. This is a battle. A battle for identity. A battle for naming rights. A battle for life. And our G-d is a warrior and a shelter. Ancestral brilliance never tried to iron out the wrinkles of G-d, the wildness of G-d, the violence of G-d like my seminary professors. G-d is warrior and weapon. G-d is parent and protector.

I bristled against their judgement of the language I heard my ancestors use truthfully and powerfully. They were at war with a culture that engaged them violently because they were Black, and for no other reason. Regardless of the socioeconomic realities my white professors had known, they would never know that war. And their desire to eliminate that language only served to hide the violence my ancestors knew then and we know now. We were realists and we enlisted the G-d of justice to fight this war with us and to stop those who would destroy us.

Today I am singing these songs because the battle is real. There is a furor swirling about teaching the history of my ancestors in schools across the length and breadth of this nation. I hear these songs again because another army is rising up, seeking to visit a second, permanent death upon my ancestors by erasing their stories or by refashioning them in the interest of white rule and the myth of a linear American progress toward justice. The numbers are growing in this crumbling house of those who are pouring the putrid from an ancestral pitcher.

Wade Morris and Chara Bohan call this putrid outpour "mint julep" history. It is a sweetened, intoxicating brew that embodies what William Edward Burghardt DuBois called "the propaganda of history." During the late nineteenth and early twentieth centuries, textbooks were written, marketed, and sold to Southern audiences in the name of white ancestors they clung to because they believed torrents of truth would not be allowed to wash away the foundation of the Southern wing of the American house. No way. No how. These textbooks told a different story about human bondage, about John Brown, John Wilkes Booth, Abraham Lincoln, and Nathan Bedford Forrest. The violence done to ancestors and to us all by mint julep histories is inestimable. Lies that have shaped us are muscularly asserting themselves again, fueled by ancestral energy fighting to keep the status quo in place. But these mint julep histories erect dams that can only hold back the waters of truth for a limited time. The dam is breaking. The house is crumbling. Who is being called on now? The ancestors. The ancestral playbook.

"The nation," wrote historian David Blight in "'Mint Julep' History Books Influence Northern Depictions of Historical Events," an article published on Georgia State University's website, "was willing to sacrifice its historical memory (with particular emphasis on race) in the name of reconciliation." But who was reconciled? Not Indigenous people. Not Black people. This sacrifice of historical memory is not bloodless. From the funding of public policies that lead to death, death ensues. Now mixologists are pouring a deadly cocktail whose recipe was given to them by ancestors.

* * *

The battle in the crumbling American house is real. And I want to know whose pictures get hung on the wall. Who gets rooms and furniture named after them? Who has the luxury of reclining on the porch and who is sweating in the kitchen?

I hope you join me in beginning to wrestle with ancestral power both in the light and in the shadows. I hope you join me in reckoning with the spiritual reality that there are powers animating our politics and supporting or sabotaging our ability to build something new amid the wreckage of this house. Their name is ancestor. I know you see the floor buckling. You look up and see myriad holes in the roof. No matter the distractions of consumption and entertainment and mixology and playbooks that are potent, you and I cannot unsee this disrepair. No matter how hard we try.

The ancestors celebrated by those invested in keeping this dilapidated house are those who told us this is the best house in the neighborhood. But we know better, and we see better. They keep putting carpet over missing floorboards and forcing our siblings to continually mop up the filth regurgitated by their toilets overflowing detritus. Why do they stay in this house? There is but one answer. Power. Some people are growing richer and more powerful because of existing conditions.

But we who see and we who have a vision must tear this house down in order to rebuild an abode from the ground up—where there is plenty good room for us all.

The ancestors that are revered in this American house are those who further certain myths about who America was and is. These are the ones whose robes have been washed clean in the blood of the many for the interest of the few. Their images are everywhere. Their names are known beyond death, although many have forgotten their deeds. Their energy vibrates down our streets, across our states—everywhere—particularly in the streets of Washington, DC. As this federal city was made in the image of how powerful, white Americans thought themselves to be, it is marked by signs, symbols, and images of the Lost Cause, imperial expansion and conquest, and the subjugation of humans on behalf of the acquisition of power, land, and capital. A confused capital can only tell a story of a confused nation. Martin Luther King Jr. here and John C. Calhoun there. The Center for American Progress here and the US Chamber of Commerce there. What is the inner life of such a nation? Whom does it worship? And who is welcome?

We are who we venerate. We will never exceed the moral imagination of the ancestors whose lives and stories we hold sacred. America is committed to upholding the legacies and stories of those who restricted movement in the American house, those who avariciously squeezed life and labor and land from human beings, and who created an economy that cheerleads greed, hoarding, and calls kleptocracy meritocracy.

Yes, there are legions, inspired by ancestors arrayed in garments of light and love—for the battle is by, for, with, and in love—who fight this American house reality and witness the crumbling. But we who fight the fight are tiring and it seems that our successes are easily swallowed up by the political and economic machinations of the status quo.

Those who advocate that we forget these ancestors who dwell in the shadows of the American house must be called out. To fight a fight in love by not naming those who pull us away from our highest and best selves is to rewrite history. As painful as those names are, they must be remembered. Their three-dimensional stories must be told. But they must be told as cautionary tales. They must be told as an extension of our commitment to not recreate in our day the dehumanizing havoc they left in their wake. We must know who they were and know that their energy still exists. There are millions who pay obeisance to them and millions who lift them up as lights to follow. But they lead us to the shadows, where mayhem grows stronger in the absence of the light.

Why can't we fix the house? What is going on? We have to name the names who have brought us to the crumbling of the house as well as name the names of those who build a house of love, for everyone to be welcome in the house. Names like Mary McLeod Bethune, Ella Josephine Baker, and Fannie Lou Hamer and others—journalists, changemakers, theologians, organizers, economists, preachers, and politicians who get us to a place of flourishing without the loss of any of the beautiful humans that make us who we are. The stubborn, violent, and protective systems of the American house that deny us democracy and shared abundance must crumble, as must the inner life of America that cowers in fear in a corner of exceptionalism and self-righteousness, growling at and biting those who would coax it on the path of rigorous love and mutual trust.

The inner life of America is paralyzed by fear that is calcified by zero-sum mathematics. If this group prospers, it believes—as did its ancestors before—there is less for us. If you win, I lose. If you are free to live your life, you diminish my ability to control and judge you in the interest of my own superiority. Politics are driven by fear, and the bellows that keep the flames blazing gather air from demographic anxiety around a loss of control. Frankly put, America is terrified of freedom even as it cloaks itself in the language of liberty. America is always creating definitions around which human beings are not human in the American house, which are expendable, and which human logs are placed on the fires of fear.

This fear is triumphantly cheered on and nurtured by ancestors who grow more powerful in the shadowy places they call home. We know them by name. And we know them by the garments they wear. We need to be able to recognize them by both. To know what animates the books they left, the institutions they created, the politics they bequeathed, the theologies they crafted, and the legal and jurisprudential systems they engineered to protect this fear-based political economy, one they call "just" and "equal."

When I first read Richard T. Hughes's book *Myths America Lives By*, I felt like I was having a conversation with my teachers and ancestor intellectual interlopers. In the book, Hughes lays out what Black people and many others uninvited into America's house know in their bones: America is adept at deceiving itself. America is surprised by its penchant to do evil. America propagates myths to salve what remains of conscience. These myths are the blinking lights that alert us that shadowy ancestors are near, doing their work of keeping truth at bay, and managing, at a deep spiritual level, the investment in the status quo.

According to Hughes, the myths include these: America is the chosen nation, America is a Christian nation, America is the land of possibility—fueled by capitalism, and America is an innocent nation.

This mix of myths is lethal, ancestral, and violent.

These myths are not just the province of the religion of whiteness and those seeking entrance into that religion's holy temple. Black people are reliable evangelists of these myths. Minoritized people are reliable evangelists of these myths. And even those among us who know how these myths are deployed to keep us down refuse to trouble or challenge them.

I am not anti-myth. Human beings crave myths and need myths to order our lives. I am against *these* myths. They keep millions who live in America's house from taking a cleansing, transformational, liberative look at America's house.

My grandparents taught me. I know better. The Black family, communities, and cultures that reared me taught me to revere our elders. That training is deeply lodged within me. As is ancestor venerating. Growing up in these communities, ancestors were everywhere. Pictures. Stories. Institutions. Documents. As I wrote earlier, there was something in us or over us that venerated ancestors but refused to name the practice what it was. We are ancestor drenched but also ancestor phobic in very real ways. It's time for an end to this trepidation.

Boldly naming and venerating those who live among us and make facing tomorrow a sweeter thing because they walk into the future with us is essential to our life. As is teaching our children this veneration so that they will not fall prey to the dangerous mythologies that would name them as other than human. These ancestors give us stories of light and love by which to order our lives and this precious, fragile world.

Too long we have listened to the managers of America's house who policed ancestors and violently expelled those who did not comport with the aforementioned mythologies. Black people also expel ancestors. And the ancestors we expel are often those whose capacity to lead us toward light is most profound. No longer can we police our ancestors to keep white people comfortable, police our ancestors to keep ourselves solidly mainstream. As OutKast reminds us in *ATLiens*, the problem with the mainstream is that most of us are floating face down in it. Only when we stop policing the presence of our ancestors who speak truth to power and who scare America's house will liberation for us and for this nation come.

We must shout the names. Shout the name of Nat Turner, who embodied freedom. Call the name of Malcolm X, El-Hajj Malik El-Shabazz. He believed in liberation for all. We must fill our homes and institutions with images of Harriett Tubman and call her name—spy, soldier, freedom warrior. We must call the name of Elizabeth Freeman, Mumbet—who sued for the right to her own body in the eighteenth century.

It was the name of the ancestor who changed my values and my ethics. I did not begin my journey away from the Black version of white evangelicalism until I encountered and venerated new ancestors. I did not discover the Jesus of the gospels until I met ancestors who demanded that I read the Jesus of the gospels differently and faithfully. I did not seek beyond liberalism, neoliberalism, and the conflation of Black politics with Democratic Party politics until ancestors talked to me through their books and recorded lectures. Until I met their students who knew their writings and honored their names. Ancestral interactions caused scales to fall from my eyes. Where I was lost. How am I to be found. Where I was blind. How to see. These ancestors were divine agents calling me toward my truest self. Beyond the distractions and illusions designed to America's house asleep.

These divine agents aren't only the names I call. These ancestors are naming me, giving me new names. Calling me. Their call is getting louder, clearer. As I hear them, I am learning to answer.

4

Shadow Ancestors

WHEN ENTERING NEW spaces we all make sensory assessments. What does this place smell like? What do I hear? What do I see? How do I feel? This is what human beings do. We also make assessments beyond the physical senses. That's when words may fail us. But we know beyond the senses. Some places have spiritual energies that repel us, as if a force field exists in the liminal space between walking in and staying out. Other places feel extraordinarily hospitable, as if they have been waiting to embrace us. If you've ever walked into a space and felt an inexplicable jolt of harmful energy race through your body, more than likely, that jolt of energy is very much explainable. We just often choose to ignore what we know more deeply than words, feel more deeply than the physical senses.

America's house and culture thrives on choosing not to know. Choosing not to pay attention to our inner lives and the inner lives of the communities and institutions that shape the contours of our existence. This choosing to not know is dangerous. Some ancestors help us break through the numbness of our self-imposed ignorance. James Baldwin is one ancestor who comes to mind. These ancestors hold mirrors up to us and pry us away from celebrating self-deception. They show us what connects us to one another and all creation. They never let us forget that a new world marked by joy and justice is possible. Not somewhere in the future. Right. Now.

When we pierce the veil that separates life in this realm from life in the next, something glorious happens. Temporal orthodoxies and systems that have held us captive by claiming themselves to be eternal will be revealed as the shams they are. The apostle Paul's poetry stands the test of time: The glass through which we now see dimly will be crystalline. Partial knowledge will fall away and Truth will emerge. For in that new life, the need for those fig leaves that once allowed us to hide from ourselves are fewer. Yet leaves are abundant, for good, and for the healing of the nations. When we see things as they are. When we will know as we are known, we also will realize we still have choices to make.

The beauty of the apocalyptic literature of scripture is that in no uncertain terms it tells us that wars break out even in heaven. In this realm of the Ancient of Days, peace cannot be promised. Even in heaven some creatures refuse to fall into the terrifying love of G-d. They decide, even in the place where faith is no longer necessary because knowledge is complete, to cower in fear, to lurk in shadows, to harm others. Revelation says there is no need for sun or moon there. Presence is so blazingly brilliant that it lights the celestial, yet, even there, some will always feverishly search for shadows. Even there, some seek to manufacture death, maybe especially so, when life is dancing so seductively. In this realm, beyond the veil, there are ancestors who chose shadow.

Ancestors are human energy beyond time and space. Human energy always has the power to decide light or shadow, life or death. That is why whenever I enter spaces—whether a cozy home or a verdant park—I scan for the ancestral. I learned to do that from the very first, as Vinnie watched over the house, eyes on me, teaching me.

In each space I am always asking a seminal question: "What ancestral work is being done here?" For whom are these streets named? Where are the statues this community looks to? What are the mascots and whose nicknames are thrown on jerseys? After whom are these schools named? I am always on the swivel aware of the shadow ancestors in these places still stoking fear. They know the truth, yet they refuse to be free, and they seek to bind and shadow others.

Shadow ancestors play at the corners of New York City's Wall Street where two streets from the stock exchange once sold human beings. Their progenies have innovated fresh shadow ways to avoid paying for labor. And by doing so have thoroughly financialized the economy. They strip companies of their value, just another way of saying they hollow out human lives. They bundle everything from homes to loans into instruments to drive up "value" through speculation and manipulation. They dream of new ways, in the words of hip-hop collective Wu-Tang Clan, "to get cream" while avoiding the bloody truth of what their obscene wealth costs the rest of us. What they are doing is legal, celebrated, catastrophic, and the legacy of shadow ancestors. And soon there will be no value left to extract.

It's no coincidence that this energy—connecting the historical buying and selling of humans to the buying and selling of human beings now—finds its home in the same space. These ancestors know where to set up shop. They know where humans are willing to pay steep prices for power and lucre. And they know how to cloak the machinations of death in the garments of meritocracy and economic progress.

Space. Shadow ancestors occupy space. They inhabit the land. They settle in buildings. Stop. Look. Listen. Pay attention or you'll miss the places where the metaphysical manifests perceptibly. Our stuckness is aided by powers that too many believe are make-believe, even as they share space with shadows. These are not some silly "Adventures of Scooby-Doo" ghouls, but principalities, ancestors, powers of biblical proportion, forces beyond the physical realm that drive us like herds of swine toward cliffs of mutual destruction. They might gladly push us off, but some rush themselves off the cliffs.

Many deny the power of ancestors. But savvy politicians don't make speeches without summoning them. Smart corporations use their images and music and words to sell anything and everything. Preachers like me would die a thousand deaths before failing to bid ancestors to come through text and sermon. Museums depend upon ancestral pull to fill their halls. Sophisticated music venues thrust ancestral images before us to seduce us to come listen to ancestors speak to us musically from beyond the veil.

Those who would deny the power of ancestors choose spiritual ignorance at their soul's and community's peril. Beyond the intellect and beyond the gut, ancestral energy connects the humanity in us with the humanity of our forebears. Ancestral energy connects the divinity in us with the divinity in our forebears. Death has not destroyed the human and divine energy of ancestors. And shadow ancestors remain with us still. Kneading us as biscuit bakers knead dough, shaping and squeezing human beings into something to be devoured. These ancestors are capable of whipping up crippling violence. Deny their power at your peril.

Richmond, Virginia, served as a capital of the Confederacy. Those who worshiped at the church of the Lost Cause left iconography and totems everywhere. The inner life of the Confederate States of America yet throbs there with intensity. The children there remain faithful to the ancestral church. Make no mistake, Richmond wants you to know that you are in Richmond. Not Boston. Not New York. Not Chicago. Not even Atlanta or Raleigh. But Richmond.

Dotting Richmond are schools, statues, and monuments, all crafted for the sake of memory and marking space as belonging to the spiritual progeny of ancestors. Ginter Park Elementary School. James Ewell Brown (Jeb) Stuart Elementary School (renamed Barack Obama Elementary School almost a century after its founding). John B. Cary Elementary

School. Binford Middle School. Robert E. Lee Memorial Bridge. General Mahone Highway. Confederate Avenue.

Until 2020 other shrines stood watch over the city. Here is a list of Richmond's Confederate monuments that have been removed: Confederate Soldiers and Sailors Monument, J. E. B. Stuart Monument, Jefferson Davis Monument, Matthew Fontaine Maury Monument, Richmond Howitzer Monument, Stonewall Jackson Monument, Williams Carter Wicker Monument, and the Joseph Bryan statue.

These tangible remembrances are about heritage, I have heard people say, not hate. Traitorous people lived, died, and were born again in honor. This is a heritage not to be celebrated but remembered. We must never forget the lengths to which human beings will go to protect the shadow power of ancestors. They will abandon all other allegiances to preserve it.

* * *

Once my brilliant wife and I were on a local television program with Ben Jones, the actor who played Cooter Davenport on *The Dukes of Hazzard* television show. On Friday nights in the eighties it seemed like everybody watched that show, I among them, eagerly consuming the blockbuster despite its Confederate iconography. We were discussing the legacy of the Confederacy after one of America's racialized traumas resurfaced, temporarily grabbing headlines and spawning think pieces.

With clear pride, Mr. Jones spoke of his heritage. I listened. And I respectfully shared that his was a legacy built and nurtured on anti-Black white supremacy. Then I shared these quotes:

> *But not to be tedious in enumerating the numerous changes for the better, allow me to allude to one other though last, not least. The new constitution has put at rest, forever, all the agitating questions relating to our peculiar institution African slavery as it exists amongst us; the proper status of the negro in our form of civilization. This was the immediate cause of the late rupture and present revolution. Jefferson in his forecast, had anticipated this, as the "rock upon which the old Union would split." He was right. What was conjecture with him, is now a realized fact.*

> *Our new government is founded upon exactly the opposite ideas; its foundations are laid, its cornerstone rests, upon the great truth that the negro is not equal to the white man; that slavery, subordination to the superior race, is his natural and normal condition. This, our new government, is the first, in the history of the world, based upon this great physical, philosophical, and moral truth. This truth has been slow in the process of its development, like*

> *all other truths in the various departments of science. It has been so even amongst us. Many who hear me, perhaps, can recollect well, that this truth was not generally admitted, even within their day. The errors of the past generation still clung to many as late as twenty years ago. Those at the north, who still cling to these errors, with a zeal above knowledge, we justly denominate fanatics.*

Mr. Jones asked, "Where did these quotes come from?"

"This is your heritage, good sir," I said.

To this Jones said nothing.

I told him these are the words of Alexander Hamilton Stephens, vice president of the Confederate States of America from his Cornerstone Speech in Savannah, Georgia in 1861. Later Stephens backpedaled from these statements, but they were presented as a reflection of his thought concerning secession and anti-Black, white hegemony during that heated time.

Arrested for rebellion against the United States, the racist traitor was later released, elected to Congress, and after some time, became governor of Georgia. This, after taking up arms against his country. How is this possible? He worshipped at the altar of the shadow ancestors. And now Confederacy in the name of figures like Lee and Stephens creates men and women who violently desecrate the Capitol Building of their own government believing that they will pay no cost and suffer no consequences. Among those responsible for the events of January 6, 2021, may be those who will rise on the national political stage.

Men like Mr. Jones may not be familiar with Alexander Hamilton Stephens nor his pungent rhetoric, but Alexander Hamilton Stephens knows men like Mr. Jones. Stephens's rhetoric will soon find them, even if the one conveying the words comes to them from a middle-aged Black preacher. Mr. Jones and his ilk may choose to ignore truth, may tussle with the interpretation of Stephens's words, may say that the words are taken out of context. They may rally around another, fake news, flag.

But be assured of this, we are who we venerate. We are who we worship. If we think that the idolization of Confederates and the Confederacy is spiritually and morally neutral, we delude ourselves. Though we may not understand every nuance of meaning accorded to the symbols we hoist and wear and tattoo upon our bodies, the intent of those symbols works its way into our very bones and being. The words that built our ancestral houses, as Stephens's words built the Confederacy, don't have to be known by us in order to powerfully dictate our values, ideology, and ethics. These words may be all the more potent for their being hidden, working in the shadows, warping the inner lives of ignorant adherents. And endangering us all.

According to *The Washington Post*, not one large, connected, white contractor wanted to take Confederate monuments down in Richmond. They knew that they would be visited by death if they touched these holy monuments, still radiating the spiritual energy of those who placed them in Richmond. They knew there are so many ways to die, including socially. Invitations to parties or baptisms or bar (or bat) mitzvahs or to summer on Kiawah Island would be rescinded. They would be isolated islands in the ocean of affluence. They would die financially. A financial pox would be placed upon their houses. Partnerships would disappear, contracts would wither, and creditors would disappear. What kind of contractors turn down work on this order? Those who know the wrath of shadow ancestors is real.

The governor of the Commonwealth of Virginia had his chief of staff call upon Devon Henry, a Black man. Team Henry Enterprises, Mr. Henry's construction company removed twenty-four Confederate monuments in Virginia and North Carolina. To do so meant he endured death threats. Employees abandoned him. He was warned his future in business would be over. When a white contractor engaged in similar work in Louisiana, he also endured death threats, and his car was set aflame. The white contractor quit the work. Henry didn't. His wife and children supported him, though they were all imperiled.

Wearing a bullet proof vest, carrying a concealed weapon, he tore from earth the physical manifestations of shadow ancestral energy alongside faithful colleagues.

In life, the persons honored by these fallen totems once fastened to earth had violently rearranged space and people in the interest of controlling labor and land. Traitors, secessionists, enslavers, soldiers. Complex human beings who, like other American imperialists, including their enemies to the north, refused to conceive of a truly free, just, and equitable society for all humans. They were the Confederate States of America at war against the United States of America. Still very much American, with all the bloody, brutal tenets of the American empire.

Some of them were elite "planters" who did not plant and "farmers" who did not farm. They sacrificed scores of dispossessed, hardscrabble white people on countless battlefields and in the day-to-day slaveocracy that made white labor almost worthless. To this day the children of these poor whites have not rebounded economically. The planters and farmers of yore and their descendants ensure that anti-Blackness keeps the masses of white people from seeing the actual source of their economic and cultural misery. They have convinced these struggling human beings of the escalating value of the wages of whiteness. Soon, prayerfully, kingdomly, these masses will learn that whiteness does not fill bellies or souls.

Is it any wonder, when the land still bears their names, images, and spiritual energy that many devotees of the Confederacy and aligned ideologies would be responsible for Mother Emanuel, Charlottesville, and January 6, 2021? Who knows what will happen by the time these words reach you, reading this book? These who are in an ancestral legacy of "farmer" and "planter" belong to the dominant culture psychologically mesmerized by white skin, yet they are among the dominated.

Those umbilically tethered to this mythology, this ancestral energy, are locked in prisons from which neither contemporary desolation nor historical truth can free them. Even should they desire liberation, they know the peril of standing in the way of shadowy ancestors in Richmond or elsewhere. No white firm dared touch these icons. And being white never spared anyone from the death unleashed by whiteness.

On January 2, 2023, *The Washington Post* reported,

> *Over and over, history-minded friends directed [Devon] Henry to the words of John Mitchell Jr., the civil rights pioneer and editor of the Richmond Planet, a groundbreaking African American newspaper. In 1890, the year the state erected an enormous statue of Robert E. Lee on what would become Monument Avenue, Mitchell wrote about the resilience of the Black person in society. "The Negro . . . put up the Lee monument," Mitchell wrote, "and should the time come, will be there to take it down."*

Black labor placed these monuments in the ground. Black labor removed them. But why should this be the case? Why should Mr. Henry risk his life and the lives of his family to do a job no white contractor would do? When they count the cost of engagement, they err on the side of protecting themselves and the ancestral systems that bind us and inhibit our flourishing. They decline their difficult moral and ethical responsibility and pass the buck to the Mr. Henrys of the world.

Why would we ever trust powerbrokers in the United States to change, to do the work of toppling and removing? They know what exists on the other side of that ancestral showdown and they have chosen stasis. Will they topple and remove exploitative capitalism? Will they topple and remove oligarchy, plutocracy, and kakistocracy masquerading as democracy? Will they topple their ancestral white nationalism and fascism clad in garments they call Christianity? History shows that they won't. And the contemporary moment only proves that they will shapeshift, repackage, and rename the same diabolical structures their shadowy ancestors imposed upon the masses.

Where does hope reside? In a bottom-up press toward a way of being together that is more lovely, more beautiful, more just. I work in Mr. Frederick Douglass's city. The grand old man was right: Power concedes nothing without a demand. It never has. It never will. Those who are custodians of empire—from the left or from the right—will do what conscientious custodians do. They will keep the empire shiny and smelling good through crafty rhetoric and emotionally engaging optics. One thing they will not do is condemn the house that makes flourishing impossible for the teeming masses.

Here's where hope resides—and what these forebears lurking in the shadows of our existence hate—the coming together of the exploited. The shadows crushed Nathaniel Bacon's Rebellion in Virginia. They refused to allow Indigenous people, Europeans, and Africans to knit together power arrangements based upon abundance instead of scarcity. And they introduced the biological farce of race to drive a permanent wedge between those whom G-d and nature champion: common human beings. Racial ideologies, as manifest economically, politically, and theologically, are based upon the lie of scarcity. Shadow ancestors and those who venerate them are taking what belongs to you. These people are moving into your spaces, engorging themselves with more money and power, while the regular folk, the workaday people, are fighting the vitriol.

Like it is a Broadway play, I see this choreographed status quo dance time and time again in city government and federal government. The marks are on the stage. Everyone knows where to go. The actors know their lines. The dancers know their positions.

America doesn't need one more politician telling this nation it is the greatest nation on earth. America doesn't need one more preacher on the empire's payroll telling this nation that G-d has chosen it. America needs millions of citizens to hold up a mirror to ourselves and to or body politic. America needs the ancestors who before us have demanded a politics that is not for sale, who demanded an economy that does not operate on the reverse Robin Hood principle, who demanded theologies where G-d is not made in the image of the wealthy, white, and well-connected, who demanded an ancestral accounting.

* * *

Descendants, we can create something different. We can do something different. All our sociopolitical and economic orthodoxies are not truths set forth from the foundation of the world.

There is so much light around us, but we are positioned so that we cannot see it. We have been acculturated to dimness. We complain that there is no light, but the light has not abandoned us, those are shadow ancestral hands blocking it. Consent, as Noam Chomsky said in the book *Manufacturing Consent* that he coauthored with Eward Herman, is being manufactured. We capitulate to this dimness because we are trained to do so. Those statues blocked so much light. Even when statues are gone, the shadow that planted them there remains.

Ancestral realities are at war in our time. The forces of freedom are aligned against the forces of fascism. The forces of salvation are arrayed against the armies of the status quo. There is a showdown between shared abundance and capitalism. Crumbling empires are facing off against new ways of imagining justice, truth, and political economy. We must choose sides. My elders, now ancestors, would often say, "God can't use no coward-soldiers!" This is a victory that can be won. But not without fighting.

Systems of death have concretized around us and atop us. We must press toward the light and through the concrete. I remember the first time I stopped to notice plant life growing through concrete near my grandmother's house. Concrete appears to be solid when viewed by the naked eye. But it's filled with countless microscopic cracks. Our economic system's cracks are no longer microscopic. Our political cracks are cavernous, gaping holes. Our theological cracks are elephantine. And through these cracks a thousand flowers are blooming.

Many are compelled, as I am, to struggle in flawed, yet committed ways to midwife that which is grown by light and emerges through the cracks throughout the world: new ways of sharing life and love in the interest of all, not just some. While shadow ancestors and those who pay them obeisance thought that slabbing layer after layer of concrete on top of us would keep us in our places, keep us from thriving, keep us from growing, the microcracks are myriad and our ancestors have always grown through them, as we have also. We find a place to sink our sturdy ancestral roots, and we push into and through the slabs all around us.

Listen, ancestral hands are extended in our direction. They beckon us out of the shadows and into the marvelous light. Many have accepted these hands in the past, hands that helped to bring us closer to G-d's beautiful dream for humanity.

It will cost something to grasp the ancestral hands reaching out for us. These hands trespass space and time to stir our spirits and bodies to be about building something new. We know that making G-d's dream for creation come true will be met with stiff opposition. Those who derive power from how we order society will use every means available to them to stop our progress. But the ancestors demand that we risk what is necessary for the dawn of a new day. Weak resignation to the status quo is unacceptable.

As I reflect on the language of ancestors, buried within it was the steady rhythm of risking life and joy in a hostile environment. They would sing, "Walk together children, don't get weary!" In other words, risk community as you build a new world. They would pray, "Like Nehemiah, we are on the wall, and we cannot come down!" In other words, risk everything to continue the work that has begun. Risk exists alongside the possibility of living into what is possible together. Many ancestors knew the risk was worth taking. And sometimes at the greatest of costs.

Grasping these hands is not without risk. Ida B. Wells-Barnett accepted these extended hands as she wrote the truth about lynching, a practice unbroken to the present day. Her life was threatened, but she preferred a life of journalistic truth-telling and the risk that followed to a life of safety and resignation to things as they were. And Jarena Lee grasped these hands and determined that women as well as men were called to be heralds of G-d's gospel. She proclaimed strongly where a man's preachment was failing, and she was authorized to keep preaching a new world into existence.

These hands are extended in my direction and in yours, beckoning us march sunward, to wrestle against shadows, to break those cracks open with the brightest light.

5

Legacy

ONCE WHEN MY aunt told me a humorous family story involving my grandfather, now an ancestor, Henry Orlando Lamar Sr., I also learned the word *haints*. Henry was the eldest of eight siblings born to Big Daddy (William N. Lamar Jr.) and Big Momma (Bessie Pitts Lamar). A fair amount of good-natured taunting and playful tormenting marked the sibling relationships my grandfather (mostly) enjoyed. Though he most certainly did not enjoy one particular walk through the woods in the late 1930s or early 1940s. As my aunt told the story about Bub (the nickname his siblings gave him), she said, he traversed the lush forests of Jones County, Georgia, headed back home. Stationing themselves strategically along the path to scare the life out of him were his younger siblings.

Walking alone, he met forests that were foreboding. His siblings hid behind trees and under vegetation as they simulated the eerie, guttural, otherworldly sounds of haints.

As my aunt told the story, she doubled over into joyous laughter that danced right on the edge of pain. She cried, "Bub thought the haints were riding him!"

Haints are malicious spirits trapped in transit between the worlds of the living and the dead. Haints have a sordid rap sheet. They were thought to kidnap children and engage in other mischief. Africans bequeathed the idea of haints to their progeny here in America. I wish I knew the haint stories my grandfather and his siblings were told by their elders to protect them from evil and of course to limit their own proclivities toward troublesome behavior. I can only imagine. Sometimes in the stillness of the night, I can hear my great-great grandmother Panola Norman Lamar sharing haint stories with her beloved offspring.

Ridden by haints and seized by fear, my grandfather took off running through the woods. I carry this story with me. It is tucked away in my pocket. It's the story that helps to explain how I feel living and working in Washington, DC. I love Washington. I hate Washington.

In this town, this turbulent seat of imperial power, I am always being ridden by haints. They attach themselves to me. I feel their presence not only spiritually, but physically. Monuments to those who would never have acknowledged my grandfather's beauty or my grandmother's brilliance are breeding grounds for haints. Streets named for enslavers and conquerors are places where spirits that would do mischief among us congregate and keep us tethered to the inhumane world imagined by their namesakes who aimed to keep human beings from thriving and reaching the height of their glory. In DC haints riddle spaces and places with the names of those who did so much harm and whose legacies have been unrelentingly violent.

We exist in a world alive with spiritual energy. We have been trained to value things that are physical or that neatly comport with scientific ways of knowing. I reject this tyranny of interpretation. The world is alive with powers we do not see and cannot quantify. The story of the haints is humorous and it is grounding. I never ignore the spiritual energy that I experience in people, places, or things. That energy takes residence in us. It made my grandfather run. It agitates others differently. Sometimes it freezes those who would otherwise act.

I first felt the haints of Washington, DC, riding my back in 1990, as I was on the way from a family reunion. I was mourning. My beloved grandmother, Sallie Green Lamar, had died in March 1989. This ancestor remains a fount of pure joy. Together we watched baseball and, in the kitchen, I licked cake batter from her mixing bowls. She gave me dollar bills and bear hugs. I feel them now. She was the first person in my life to die whom I loved deeply. Hers was the first corpse I touched, her soft brown cheeks turned cold and hard. She had been dead for about eighteen months by the time we had our family reunion. I kept seeing her, but she wasn't there. I kept hearing her, but she wasn't speaking. It was really tough and continues to inform how I see the world today. I was withdrawn. I was in my head. I was mad as hell.

I was preoccupied with the inanity of death. I still am. How does this even work? One day you see someone and the next day they are gone. One day their voice and energy fill rooms and hearts and then they disappear in the way that dubious exegetes speak of the rapture. A lot was going on in my soon-to-be sixteen-year-old body and mind at the time. In retrospect, I think I both avoided and wrestled with grief by becoming more politicized. It was 1990 and I delved deeply into golden age hip-hop. Chuck D declared that only a nation of millions could hold us back. KRS-One laid down his philosophy of the industry. And I was in my own fight with death and life and with the emergence of ideas that formed and continue to inform how I see the world today.

The haint of grief grew inside of me, trapping me between the unfolding of this world and the mystery of the next, which had laid claim to my grandmother. And then when I was fourteen, we arrived in Washington. There, I grew angrier by the day. I saw no liberty. I sensed no justice. All I saw were buildings that sat on stolen land. I saw buildings constructed by the labor of the enslaved. I saw pretty language written in Latin and English that had hardly ever seeped into the actual workings of the political economy that constrained millions domestically and shackled many abroad.

The shadow haints danced all around me. They wore wigs like Washington and Jefferson. They played chess with the lives and bodies of my ancestors to "save" the Union like Lincoln. They cut us out of the largesse of much of the New Deal like Roosevelt. I despised what I saw and what I felt.

Together with my family I toured Congress and the Supreme Court. I was with them physically, but mentally I was running like my grandfather through dense, spirit-infested woods in Washington. What I heard were screeches and screams designed to frighten me from haints, stuck between this world and the next, shadows who knowingly constructed a nation designed to siphon life, liberty, and happiness from us. The louder they screamed the angrier I became.

Smiling tour guides arrayed in uniforms devised to keep them from passing out in the brutal Washington heat and humidity would not respond to my questions about who built the White House and majestic government buildings on Capitol Hill. They were irritated by my curiosity. So were the other white folks on their pilgrimage to the Mecca of their civil religion. The voices of the haints grew louder as I kept peppering them like a lawyer confronting a hostile witness on the stand. I quoted the histories that I had read. I gave facts, figures, and dates. The tour guides kept to their hagiographic script. I jabbed. I was unrelenting, punching haints and pushing through to the light of truth.

I could not have known that thirty-four years later I would be serving as the pastor of Metropolitan African Methodist Episcopal Church in that same troublesome city. Metropolitan sits on the longest continuously held parcel of land owned by persons of African descent in the District of Columbia. Our very existence disturbs the shadow haints that hang around Washington. We've been on this land and in this church since our founding in 1838 and we are not going anywhere.

Mama Itihari Touré, one of my mentors and sages, calls Metropolitan an ancestral shrine. She speaks elegantly of the energy she feels bursting through every pew, brick, and pane of stained glass in our sanctuary.

I have written and spoken in many media outlets of what happened to our church at the hands of the Proud Boys. The energy of our church, our holy ancestral shrine, calls out to those who would do damage to us or any other human beings. The ancestors from this shrine invite others into something more lovely, into the way of life. Our energy says yes to beauty, humanity, justice, and joy. It is not manipulated by fear or coercion. We have stood where we are, amongst the haints, since the 1880s. The Proud Boys tried to kill our energy. So have many others before them. It cannot be killed. It will not die.

I see my grandfather running through Jones County's forests with haints riding his back, unsure of every step, yet, for the joy set before him, determined to return to hearth and home. That is my legacy. Each generation has been making its way through forests, panting and trusting. And some of us don't make it home. Some of us don't get to hear the laughter and feel the love of trickster siblings at the end of our arduous journeys. But we run in the direction of home nonetheless. An energy that some would stop at all costs beckons us home.

I marvel at this legacy, and I have struggled for many years to gain an understanding of what powers it. What energizes this way of being human? My answer is one word. *Joy*. Stubborn joy. Determined joy. Flint-hard joy. Perspiration-soaked joy. Joy is what gets you through haint-haunted forests, despite fear, one step at a time. Joy is the only force that can get you home.

It is strange that even my discovery of haints was wrapped in a package of joy, of humor. It was after my grandfather died in 2010 that my Aunt Dot, fifteen years my grandfather's junior, recalled this story as our family gathered for his funeral. As we prepared to bid farewell to our patriarch on this side, our elders recounted joyfully his life and extended his presence among us through the veil of death. Black folk are joy weavers. I saw my ancestors take scraps of grief and gratitude, pain and possibility, death and delight, and stitch quilts that still keep us warm and catch our tears.

It has taken nearly a half-century of living for me to begin to unravel the densely layered wisdom of my ancestors. This wisdom is found in many spaces and many ways, among them ritual, religious practices, books, familial narratives, and the family reunion movement. This movement has been traced to the reality of African families in America over generations. As families were cruelly separated during enslavement, as many fled violence once chattel slavery shapeshifted into other vile institutions, keeping in touch with family was often dangerous if not impossible. Pages upon pages of Black newspapers between the 1870s to the 1930s were devoted to helping Black people find long lost parents, siblings, spouses, and children. People searched for years to renew bonds of blood and love.

What formed in danger, separation, and impossibility was the deepest of bonds. For family reunions are about joy.

The food shared. The prayers prayed. The games played. As I write, my family is planning a reunion. My extraordinary father is quarterbacking our efforts. He sent an email to family members urging their participation in the planning process of the reunion. It is a daunting task for a large gathering. The logistics are complicated, and volunteer labor is, well, volunteer labor. Something has compelled my father over the years to pick up the baton of convening us in focused fellowship. I think I know what that something is.

My father's generation was once cushioned by two living elder generations. Most of them have taken their place in that innumerable caravan. Only two elders remain. As the world convulses in so much violence and the stage appears to be set for the unraveling of the lives that we have known due to extreme politics, extreme heat, and extreme economic insecurity, my dad has been summoned to return us to the thirst-quenching waters of ancestral wells dug long ago.

What helped us to survive then was family, togetherness, and a commitment to mutual thriving. That same human technology will save us now. As the generations grow and time lengthens and space drives us farther away from familial lands, we must be careful to plan reunions that will help us to rekindle the flames of love that warm us, body and soul.

Dad emailed pictures to those of us on the planning committee. Pictures of his grandparents' generation, his great-grandparents' generation, and his great-great-grandparents' generation graced our inboxes. His words framed the images,

"Our ancestors are encouraging us and cheering us on to finish this good work we are about to begin. G-d willing, our work will produce a great harvest of love and joy. Can't you hear them, too?"

They are dead. They are alive. They are speaking. And the telos of their conversation, the end of their ancestral entreaty to us, is for us to delight in a great harvest of love and joy.

What is to come will require nothing less than our full commitment to great harvests of love and joy such as these. The desert is growing day by day and oases are not luxuries. They are the very stuff that life requires. As a much younger man, agitated by my newfound historical knowledge and political awakening and sudden grief, I wondered why my elders were not as angry as I was. Yes, I admit I was self-righteous in my Public Enemy t-shirt, Africa medallion, and high-top fade haircut. But older now, I am as awake as I ever was, even if more judicious in how I expend my energy. And I see the steady, slow genius of parents and grandparents who kept working, and cooking, and paying bills and providing me with a great harvest of love and joy that made my intellectual awakening and political impatience possible.

Their primary theological act of gathering was to provide us with a great harvest of love and joy. Their primary political act was to provide us with a great harvest of love and joy. I now know how radical that was in a place like the United States of America. They had lived what I read about, yet they were patient with my professorial accounts of what they had suffered. They made space for me so that I would commit my life to making space for others. Not just space for those related to me by blood. I was duty bound to make space for all related to me by our shared, radiant, and fragile human bond. They were revolutionaries disguised as mill workers, cafeteria workers, insurance salesmen, childcare providers, and teachers. They built worlds for us. Those worlds were so secure that we hardly knew of the haints that roamed in the forest beyond the moats of the castles of love they built for us.

The ancestors who beckon us to gather were not perfect. Yet, their energy is driven by light, not shadow. Their aim in life was not to exploit or control or conquer or pillage. They met challenges mostly in response to the overwhelming restrictions that the shadow ones put on them in life. With so much clipping their wings, yet they never cursed flying. They prayed for soaring descendants. And blessedly, marvelously, many of us are doing just that.

My father has been summoned not to just plan a family reunion, but to assist the ancestors in their work of setting tables of joy for us all. We will need to know one another more deeply to weather the storms on the horizon. To my father, family members not knowing family members is both tragedy and travesty and he aims to do something about it. When we are adrift on life's seas, family members are often those who throw out lifelines of support. I am who I am because of this communal way of building human connections.

The economy of the American empire is built around personal pursuits, and the theology of the American empire revolves around personal salvation. But in our world, that has never been the case and may it never be so. Family reunions are a practice, an ancestral practice, that makes alternative worlds possible, rooted in joy. I see this wider family reunion in the church of the ancestors where I preach. This community. This joy.

My legacy is joy. Indefatigable joy. Not happiness, which is also a lovely pursuit. But joy. I think of happiness as evaporating quickly like the mists above the lakes I knew as a child. There is a flimsiness to happiness. But joy is sturdy like a dining room table with a great crowd packed around it.

My ancestors did not leave me houses or land. I did not get a down payment for my first home, nor an account filled with quickly appreciating equities. I got joy.

I don't exactly recall when joy began to make sense to me. Maybe it is the proliferation of the idea of Black joy. The family reunions. Maybe it is the ancestral reflection that accompanies this work and the work I do as a pastor, preacher, and organizer. Something in my soul was able to connect with the joy my people took, gathered in what their minds imagined, their hands crafted, their bodies created, and their mouths spoke. They were never just surviving. They ornamented mundane things with uncommon beauty. They made scarcity act like it was abundance. We live in the world that Black joy made.

You name the cultural product, and I will show you its debt to Black joy.

This realization inevitably affected my theology. G-d's work of creation and redemption is not centered in a need to reveal human sin and insufficiency. I had preached a G-d whose only desire was to fix us. But the G-d who wants to delight with us and in us has found me. G-d seeks to reveal our bountiful beauty, which is G-d's own beauty and our limitless possibilities, which are also divine.

The poetic beauty of incarnation is that G-d cannot resist humanity. G-d fills humanity with divinity and beckons us likewise to be filled with divinity. How anyone could diminish human persons baffles and befuddles me. The spark of the divine is so evident in us all. Yet, forces are at work to extinguish that spark before it becomes a flame. And I understand those who want to kill the spark. They want to keep the world as it is. They know that if the spark ever ignites among us all we will no longer be controlled. The spell of death and scarcity will be broken. G-d's work is fanning the flames of the fire of joy that would burn in and among us all.

Joy changed my politics. I have been committed to broad-based organizing for power for many years. Broad-based organizing brings together people from different races, cultures, and faith traditions to build power in order to make change. We know that being right doesn't change policy and politics. We know that loving people and placing human interests before profit doesn't change policy and politics.

Power is the ability to make change. Too often, we have the right ideas for people and the planet, but we lack the power to change the systems that keep us from thriving together. This is a different kind of power than the power that removes power from others or greedily subsumes or shadows the good of others. Shadow ancestors and their living progeny use dominant power to keep control. It is extractive and bone-crushing. It hierarchizes dangerous mythologies of meritocracy and divine blessing. Nothing received via exploitation or oppression is ever a blessing. Blessings cannot be conveyed via boulevards soaked in blood. And the so-called blessings all around me in Washington, DC, and throughout the United States are awash in blood.

We must not be afraid of power. We have a different power and we must learn to use that power in love.

I have organized for power in Jacksonville, Florida, Prince George's County, Maryland, and Washington, DC. The only things that I have seen change our interlocking systems of government and economics are organized people and organized money. The Supreme Court has decided to pretend that floods of unaccountable money in politics do not create oligarchy, plutocracy, and kleptocracy. They are wrong. We see the evidence in local, state, and federal government. This reality can only be combatted by organized people building rich relationships and demanding that change be implemented and sustained. Policy revanchism is real. Are we paying attention to what they are doing to what we have gained?

The most basic building block to amass this power is one-on-one conversations. We have built power house by house, street by street, block by block, and neighborhood by neighborhood by having conversations at tables, in cafes, in churches, synagogues, mosques, and temples. The only sustainable power is relational power.

In the city and region I serve, through conversation power, by ancestors and practitioners alike, I am constantly reminded of something. Power must be built on a foundation of joy. The Saul Alinski model of organizing asks a resonant question, "What makes you angry?" That question is profound for those who want to see a change in their communities and in society at large. I was asked that question in my twenties when I did not yet grasp the power of joy. I believed that anger illumined the manifold problems around us, and that anger would sustain me in the glorious struggle to make a new world. I was wrong. Anger's illumination was ultimately too faint to light a constructive path to the new world I envisioned. My angry eyes saw problems but could not see clearly what was possible at the end of rage. Anger is an important emotion. But anger is a sprinter. Joy is a marathoner.

Thanks to the ancestors and practitioners, the elders and table-gatherers, we now organize for power with a joyful, creative vision of who we can be at our best, when resources flow without oppression or exploitation taking what rightfully belongs to the people.

The writer of Hebrews offers wisdom that I am just beginning to grasp. The author writes of Jesus's arduous journey toward the cross. And let me be clear, liberative theology makes no room for G-d engineering the lynching of Jesus to save humanity. Lynching is never the will of G-d. Lynching is always the will of human beings. The poetry of resurrection is that G-d is the anti-lyncher. G-d is the lynching reverser. Yet we know Jesus's life, and the lives of those committed to getting us home to justice and peace will be marked by lynchings and crucifixions designed by human beings. The biggest and most effective game that white evangelical theology and its antecedents have played on us is to make us think that G-d wills crucifixions and lynchings. From this game comes the belief that we will not question them when they lynch and crucify us. We will tell them it is G-d's will as they place nooses around our necks and nails in our hands.

Jesus knew better. And so did the ancestors who cheer us to keep running toward home. G-d did not set a cross before Jesus. And G-d does not set crosses before us. G-d sets joy before us. In Hebrews 12 we are told that Jesus endured the cross for the sake of the joy that was set before him. We can run through hell with haints riding our backs for the sake of the joy that G-d and the ancestors have set before us.

* * *

We live in a time when stating this fact forecloses conversations. But if people demand foreclosing truth to have an exchange, you know that they are invested in nothing but mendacity, nothing but lies. We cannot lend our voices or our gifts to violently obfuscatory dialogues of intentional erasure. No more Blackwashing the facts with inclusion and diversity. No more dressing up the imperial past and present with the language of democracy and the demonic theology of manifest destiny. There is no hope for this fragile project unless we allow the blood to speak.

The ancient wisdom that is scripture tries to impress upon us in the story of Cain and Abel that all homicides are fratricides, sororicides. Because we are all kin. This ancient wisdom is also clear that the Divine never allows fratricide, no matter the reason, to go unnoticed. Genesis 4: 9–11 contains some of the most important verses in Holy Writ, "Then the Lord said to Cain, 'Where is your brother Abel?' He said, 'I do not know; am I my brother's keeper?' And the Lord said, 'What have you done? Listen, your brother's blood is crying out to me from the ground!'"

Our killing machines are different than Cain's. But we kill all the same and with startling, ruthless efficiency. Our justice, economic, and health care systems slaughter many. Yet there are no fingerprints to be dusted on smoking guns and no eyewitnesses to be sussed out by gumshoe detectives. The carnage remains. New bodies fall atop the bodies of those who were sacrificed to build what many call the greatest and freest nation the world has ever known. I object. And I believe the G-d of the universe objects, too. Ask the ancestors. Ask those who are Indigenous. They left signs of their marvelousness. And the shadow ancestors left signs of their murder. Ask the Africans. They left signs of their marvelousness. And the shadows left signs of their murder. Ask poor Europeans whose labor was stolen before whiteness consolidated its power. Their marvelousness remains. They were not spared from murder by the color of their skin.

G-d asks a question. "Where is your brother?" Doesn't G-d already know? Maybe. Maybe not. Is this a question to establish fact? Or is this a question designed to pierce the human heart? Is this question designed to make Cain hear again his brother's final screams? To hear Abel's last moments when he painfully gurgled oxygen and blood and coughed out a final vile concoction? This question is designed to make Cain smell the blood and death that wafted at the scene of the crime. To taste again the results of his foul act. And G-d takes this personally. Human death is always personal to G-d. When humans die G-d dies, too. G-d says that Abel's blood cries out. Not to the universe. Not into the ether. Abel's blood cries to G-d, G-dself. Blood screams, laments, and prays. G-d hears. G-d will answer.

And hold on. What does this have to do with joy? Everything. The joy that is possible for us cannot go around the blood all around us. It goes through it. We must account for Abel. G-d demands it. We will never build what is possible among us by denying our past, painful though it may be. Therapists tell us this as individuals. The best of our faith traditions tells us this as communities. The purpose of recounting the blood is not to cripple us nor to wed us to the past. The purpose is to remember, to lament loudly and frequently, and to build a future where we will never sacrifice a single human life for any reason. That kind of future is possible. Even now. We can break the spell of death.

We can get home from here. Yes, here. Our problems are manifold and real. Ecological devastation, climate apartheid, economic inequality, fascism, homophobia, transphobia, the list is long and lengthening. I see our collective pain from my place as pastor, organizer, and community servant. I hear the blood of those slain by siblings and those slain by systems crying out to be acknowledged. That cry is only and always for the cessation of bloodshed. Blood does not cry for more blood. Blood cries for the carnage to end. Our way home is through the valley of crying blood. This is the only route by which we may learn to study war no more.

* * *

My grandfather was navigating his way home through the forests of Jones County, Georgia, in the height and heat of the Jim Crow South. His siblings still had enough light and life in them to tease and taunt him, to attempt to scare him into silliness. There is something curious about the human soul. It fights to find joy, to connect, even in the harshest of realities. Big Momma, Big Daddy, and Grandma (Big Daddy's mother) built a castle of love for their children from the 1920s through the 1950s. I am still nourished from the overflow of that love and joy a century later. And though life takes me beyond the moat that protected the castle, I can find my way home.

But I am most concerned with those who know of no castle of love. There are too many humans who have not been afforded a fortress of protection. They have been cordoned off from what my father continues to beautifully name "a great harvest of love and joy." When we realize that all of humanity is invited to the family reunion, then we will know that it is our duty and destiny to bring those outside of love's castle in. Joy is set before us. But endurance is necessary to reach the fullness of that joy.

I don't know where my grandfather set off to on that day. Had he gone to work? Was he running an errand for his parents? Maybe he went to call on my grandmother. His why is lost to history. But he intended to get home. He ventured out, but his goal was to return home. Humanity has strayed. Some of us are trying to get back home. Some of us long for home, but we feel like we were never there. Still, we want to go. And we want to bring the family with us. But the journey is not easy. The forest between us and home is filled with howling, screeching haints. Their goal is to make us think that we are already home. That what we see is the best that we can hope for or expect. That we must stop running, capitulate to fear, and make our beds where we are.

But if we are to have the future that is possible, we must soundly reject the notion that we are already home. I learned a lesson from my ancestors. When haints howl loudest is when our joy is most intense. We bring joy to family reunions and to funerals. We keep joy when running through haint infested forests. And joy sings, even after they had been wounded by the world, "And the world can't do me no harm. . . ."

6

G-d and Ancestors

WE DON'T REMEMBER being submerged in amniotic fluid in our mothers' wombs. Most of us barely remember happenings from our early childhoods. And though through the years as I age, sights and sounds and smells from that period seep through to my consciousness, it's as though through a veil. All of us experienced so much that we cannot readily grasp nor name those experiences, yet they remain foundational to who we are and who we are becoming. This is no less true for cultures, peoples, and nation states. Who we were shapes who we are and who we will be, even if we may not be cognizant of the truth of who we have been.

Like most American citizens, we may believe with religious fervor in a thoroughly propagandized account of our collective past. Though the account lacks truth or holds to shadow, it remains a mile marker by which we assess the distance we have traveled. And it is a signpost we hold to, as we name the places we have been. These mile markers and signposts are not just symbols, they are definitional. It matters not if these mile markers and signposts are anchored in the soil of truth. People will kill should their sacred mile markers and signposts be moved or questioned.

Ask the saints at Mother Emanuel. Ask the protestors at Charlottesville.

We are submerged in the amniotic fluid of the greatness of this nation. Its purity, its divine destiny, and its granting of freedom and justice to all who follow liberty's light to its hallowed shores are articles of civic faith. In my bones there is a radically different story. It is etched in my DNA. It whispers in the laughter I heard and the prayers I ear hustled in my mother's womb.

What I know is this: Every time I hear this nation's story told without the recognition of my ancestral story, violence is done. The violence of erasure.

Ancestors are the bodiless embodiments of our mile markers and signposts. And I measure the distance I have traveled from where I last encountered Big Daddy and Dada, Mommee and Nanny. These are ancestors, merciless truth-tellers, consumed with an abiding love for me. They are not interested in telling me how great I am. What they do is point me to the vistas I have yet to see and the mountains I must yet climb. And along the way, as I collect more mile markers in my rearview, they provide ancient paths and food for the journey: bread for my soul's hunger and water for my soul's thirst. That is the vigilant, ongoing work of ancestors.

Ancestors weave narrative. We come to know them through story. And ancestors are coauthors of our lives. My elders who are now ancestors have fingerprints on every page of my story. Part of my spiritual practice is to conjure them, to catalog every memory. What did they wear? Clear as crystal I see a green checkered dress my grandmother used to wear. How did they smell? My grandfather's cherry pipe tobacco was one of my favorite olfactory delights. To spend some time with him, I bought some and occasionally smoke it. He returns along with the crisp Georgia winter evenings I once knew. I hear elder laughter and ancestor chastisement. And I wonder what made them who they were, even as I have memorized the lessons they taught through the lives they led. Wonderfully human, complex, and possessed of feet of clay, I knew theirs to be the strongest of clay feet. I know because I and many others stand upon them, and they have yet to shatter under the weight.

My work here is to conjure them and to conjure those they conjured. I labor to give language to who they were and what they valued. I recognize their mastery of the arts of living, loving, and creating oases of joy in deserts of despair. Kin to them, I joyfully contemplate the many people of that generation who are still helping to write my story, which is also theirs. Continually I ask, How can I distill their wisdom for those who do not have the gift of having sat at their tables, ridden in their cars, and been caressed by the musicality of their language and laughter? Always one short sentence returns, carrying all the freight of that wisdom: Be human.

But to speak of being human, ancestor wisdom always began with the Great Ancestor. The first thing these ancestors did was to imbue their children and charges with a sense of mystery, a respect for the world beyond the material. There was something more than the world we see. That something more was benevolent. That something more had moral expectations of us. That something more was our origin. That something more was our destiny.

I would ask them, "Where did I come from?" and "Where did you come from?" The answer always was, "We came from God. God made us and God put us here." When death invaded our ranks, we went to funerals. I asked them, "Where did she go?" "God took her, baby," they would say. "She is with God."

Whether you are atheist, agnostic, or a cultured despiser of religion or spiritual systems or language (with good reason), I ask you to stay with me here. Because we all have a stake in the cosmology of mystery, beauty, and elegance, justice and community. We were taught that we were connected to all things, all creatures, and to the earth through G-d language. We were taught wonder through G-d language. We were taught that we were heir to mystery through G-d language.

Fresh vegetables would often be on my grandparents' small kitchen table. Peppers, tomatoes, and okra abounded. They had grown these good gifts. Planted, watered, weeded, and protected them at the farm Big Daddy left to them. Curious about the process, I rode my red Western Flyer bicycle down to the farm where I saw my uncles Walter and Norman in the field. "Hey, Billy," they said. "Come on over here, boy."

They worked and I watched. Then they gave me a job. My brown hands were immersed in black earth.

Over the sacred earth, they worked and talked and laughed. They told stories that transported me to places I would never see. When they got to a plant that was "puny," that had failed to thrive, they said, "I sure hope the good Lord will send some rain. We shonuff need it." And I was plunged again into mystery. Mystery put us here. Mystery took us back when we died. Mystery sent rain.

No one made an allowance for us to think that we were independent agents, that I was a rugged individual, master of my fate, or captain of my soul. I, we, were radically dependent upon a benevolent mystery we called G-d. And we were not void of responsibility. We did not wait for G-d to till the soil, plant the crops, and harvest them. That was our job. But we knew that we needed rain for our efforts to achieve their desired end. That was G-d's job.

These ancestors also ensured that our conception of G-d was thoroughly and deeply rooted in community. We never conceived of G-d apart from other humans. Ever. Church was the place where this belief took on complicated, beautiful, frustrating flesh. Sunday school. Memory verses. Easter speeches. Choir rehearsals. Tom Thumb weddings. Pageants and plays. Black History Month presentations. Ushering. Christian education trips. The list is long. But now I get it. They were teaching us that G-d work is community work. Discerning who G-d is, where G-d is, and how G-d works is for *us* to do together, not for anyone to do alone. Surely many aspects of the spiritual life are conducted in isolation from other humans, but the true test of the spiritual life, of the G-d-with-us life, is how we respond to one another in community.

My ancestors abhorred those people who claimed to know G-d but were treacherous and evil in community. They would point this out: G-d-talk was easy. G-d-walk in community was something different. Those who prayed fervently but would not lift a finger to help a human in need were suspect. Those who wanted G-d to bless America but busted unions and gave plutocrats unchecked power were suspect. White folks who built beautiful churches but kept us from what G-d intended through means of violence, unfair law, and custom were not to be taken seriously if they claimed to be lovers of G-d. The G-d-life was worked out in love for humanity and community—or it was as fraudulent as a game of three-card monte.

Through G-d language they taught us mystery and the art of living in community. They did not separate the ethereal from the ethical. Heavenly pursuits meant nothing if they were of no earthly good. G-d language has been deployed for deplorable reasons, too. But for most of human existence this language has been used to keep us humble as specks in the grandeur of creation and to keep us aware that we cannot exist apart from the many unfolding wonders that dance about us every day.

Be human. That is the sermon ancestors preach. That is the song ancestors sing. But being human does not originate in us nor with us. Being human starts beyond us. That is what religion is, a binding together of humans with cords not of our making. I celebrate every culture that has technologies for this sacred work. I do not disparage any religion, and I do not think my religion to be the final arbiter of Truth. My work is not to entice people to abandon their sacred identities to become part of mine. I will never abandon what my ancestors gave me. I celebrate all expressions of being human that do not start with us.

Being human cannot happen apart from an awareness of Mystery. We were born. We live. We die. We come again. Resurrection tries to tell this story. Reincarnation tries to tell this story. The One who returned from death's grip, in my tradition, did not go to a temple or a synagogue to pray after being raised from the dead. He went to his friends. He sent word to those whose love had failed him through those faithful women whose love knew no retreat. The resurrected Christ's first priority was to reestablish community and to prepare his friends to be human for the time he would ascend again to the ancestral realm. He walked through a door of fear and presented himself, wounds and all, bidding them peace. He talked with them and ate with them.

Mystery raised him to return to community and prepare them for life without his physical presence, but with his ongoing Presence. This is what ancestors do. They help us to become human in their present absence and in their absent presence.

The only story that can save us is the story of the divinity of humanity and the humanity of divinity. No separation. No alienation. Life that is life is fully and always aware of being permeated by mystery. To be human is to cultivate that awareness and to extend its gifts to all who share our glorious and terrible terrestrial plight.

Be human. Almost thirty years ago I was shaken by a lecture in seminary. I don't know which class. And I can't find my notebooks. But I will never lose these words. The professor said, "Eastern Christianity believes that God became human so that human beings would become divine."

I was perplexed. I was intrigued. The white evangelical colonization of my theological imagination thought, *We can't be god! That is blasphemy! We are only weak and frail humans. We are prone to sin.* And then I thought more deeply, aided by the whispers of ancestors whose theological minds knew no such pollution of their theological thinking that keeps us perpetually infantile, dependent on guilt driven preachment about who we cannot be.

What if, I heard whispered, *there was something more to being beautifully human than guilt and the need for Jesus's blood to cleanse us? What if G-d expected that we would take on divine characteristics as human beings without that maturity being dependent on the lynching of Jesus?* The ancient Eastern Christianity calls this *theosis*, the gift of taking on G-d's character and being united with G-d by the Spirit. I imagine a whole new way of being for those who would see the work of being human not as the constant purgation of guilt, but the union of humans to the Divine (and to one another) by the Spirit. The end of our colonialized preachment has been that G-d wants to cleanse us because we are unworthy. What if we preached the gospel words that G-d awaits union with humans by G-d's power so that the fullness of human possibility, union with G-d, can be real for us all?

Be human. To be human was the lesson. Each time they sent us to an elder's house with a plate of food. Each time they sent us with scraps for neighborhood pets and animals. And each time they taught us not to hate. They were specific in this injunction. They were not philosophical or esoteric. We rarely asked them about the horrors of slavery, the brutality of Jim Crow. I never knew them to outline in detail their pain and all the deprivations they experienced. They did not live under the tyranny of the therapeutic. They were not driven by expressing how they felt and experienced the world. But when the unmistakable happened. When white supremacy's violence punched squarely in the jaw, they would speak. "Don't be like white folks," they would say. "Don't have that kind of hate. Don't be like that." Never revenge. They didn't play that. But always protection. Be human.

I have never forgotten that. Being human means you're unwilling to sacrifice other humans for any purpose. White supremacy is many things. Among them, it is also a system of human sacrifice. It kills and eats and enslaves and robs and steals. My people knew this. They didn't spend a whole lot of time spinning their wheels about it, though their lives were never cordoned off from its savagery. Yet, my ancestors spent their energy being human. Every movement, every intellectual and theological attack on this kind of violence, every song sung and dance danced to move us forward was rooted in this belief. Be human.

This humanity was sourced in G-d. G-d knew us before there was a church or a bible. We knew G-d before we ever heard a sermon or sang a hymn. Creation was our cathedral. The fertile fields were our flooring. The night sky ablaze with stars was our ceiling. Birdsong preached and swaying trees clapped their hands. I wish I knew the systems of belief the ancients practiced in detail. My immediate ancestors could not recall all of what their ancestors knew. That gift had been violently denied them. But what their ancestors knew did recall them. That is the only explanation for their robust humanity.

This is the same robust humanity that produced Nat Turner's fierce love for freedom and Frederick Douglass's fierce diplomacy. The same humanity that fashioned Harriet Tubman, who was spymaster, military strategist, and Moses all in her small and mighty frame. This same humanity brought forth Elizabeth Freeman who sued for the right to own her body and prevailed in 1781. Turner, Tubman, and the others did not recall their African languages, but the culture of those languages recalled them. Each of those who lived the mystery from the ancestors was radically communal, deeply hospitable, and willing to risk life and limb for kith and kin. They were G-d-talkers, spirit conjurers, root workers, healers, spell-casters and spell breakers. In joy I celebrate all of who they were and how they survived with enough love and luminosity to light our paths even now.

Near the pink rotary dial telephone in my paternal grandparents' home was a magical, worn old bible. It was a classic. The cover was black pleather, scuffed but tough. The pages were trimmed in red, and it was filled with ornate drawings of biblical scenes populated by white people and white people alone. The book was magical because it contained the genealogy of my family.

The names of each child born and each ancestor ascended were recorded there. One of my favorite things to do was to take that holy book and hold it carefully in my little lap. Quietly, it would divulge its mysteries. Six generations of births, marriages, and deaths. Some deaths were premature. Many lives were long. We had first come, pierced this realm, in places like Round Oak, Georgia, and Gray, Georgia, and some of us made our appearance in Jones County, without the designation of an incorporated or an unincorporated municipality.

The dates stretched from the early 1800s to the 1970s. Almost two hundred years of living and dying and being reborn chronicled under the rotary phone. I never saw anyone else pick up that bible. No adult ever told us children not to touch it. That bible had an energy, a force field all its own. It communicated how it was to be treated. And it beckoned me to approach it, open it, and learn my story.

Genealogy has become commodification. Saliva is mailed all over the world in hopes that DNA science will reveal our origins. I celebrate origins while fully aware that American capitalism has created a market of our desire to know ourselves more deeply. I am thankful to know six generations of names and stories, but I want to know so much more. I read of Indigenous people who can trace their lineage through more than forty generations. That birthright belongs to us all. I should be able to trace and to know the names of those who have coauthored my life. Those who took that gift away knew full well what they were severing. Our mystery. Our humanity. Our community.

People cannot exist for long absent of story. So, where there is a narrative void, people story themselves with the narrative scraps available to them. Sometimes those scraps are toxic.

The United States is teeming with storyless people. Some of them are susceptible to fascist stories because their families, hollowed out economically and spiritually, tried to fill the story. Some are susceptible to a religion whose aim is to get individuals to paradise upon death because they have never seen a commitment to thriving human community on earth. Storyless people may, in desperation, buy vacuous narratives thrust upon them by corporate marketers and profiteers. But the products they are hawking will not replace the stories we crave.

My ancestors had a similar challenge in the American context. They had lost so much of their story. Yet, so much remained. Impulses and rhythms beyond speech and knowledge guided them. They knew how to be human and how to be present with creation. They moved through brutality and the machinations of human beings seemingly bereft of souls. They cultivated and grew joy like rice. But they also knew that they had to tether their story, what they had salvaged from it and what their spirits would not relinquish, to a narrative anchor in the wilderness in which they found themselves.

Some held to African traditional religions, some kept Islamic faith, and some became humanists, rejecting religion because they saw no community enacting the principles declared as sacred. It is probably most accurate to say that what we have in Black America is a gumbo of all these systems. And in my family, it is Black Christianity that has grounded my elders and ancestors for generations.

My ancestors tethered who they were by land and blood to the stories they heard from scripture. In doing so they created something that scholar Richard Newman calls Afro-Christianity. The church centered our existence spatially and narratively. Its gravitational pull upon me, my family, and so many others is indisputable. In this place, our foreparents reconstructed their ancestral houses. They could not go back and retrieve the names and faces of their ancestors on the continent. Those details were lost to time. What they could do, however, was stake new narrative ground for their progeny. The stories they could not recall were made flesh again in the narratives of scripture. The ancestors whose names they could not call got new names, biblical names.

When my grandfather and his contemporaries knelt at the altar of Saint Paul African Methodist Episcopal Church at 989 Morrow Avenue in Macon, Georgia, they were conjuring something powerful. They would arise from their pew in the amen corner. Their shoulders square, shoes spit shined, and eyes fixed upon something that I could not altogether see as a child. They would move purposely toward wood and cushion and genuflect. Their knees bowed and bodies bent as empty vessels before a full fountain, they would chant the prayer I have mentioned before, that multivalent ancestral prayer, so elegantly and economical: "God of Abraham, God of Isaac, God of Jacob . . ." Every Sunday, this is the prayer I heard.

They called upon G-d as the Primary Ancestor. They were praying for G-d to restore us in East Macon. The names of Abraham, Isaac, and Jacob were proxies for the names they no longer knew. This was more than a ritual, this was a call for the Divine to remember us, to put us back together again. My grandfather, Henry O. Lamar Sr., prayed this prayer. Brother Bennie Stokes prayed this prayer. Brother Willie Middlebrooks prayed this prayer. In a clear deft rhetorical move, they yoked G-d to us and us to G-d. They trafficked in the saving myth of humanity as divinity and divinity as humanity. They were asserting that G-d is inextricably and irreducibly bound to us. Could G-d be G-d without us, the crown jewel of creation? And what are we without the Divine?

They were declaring, "God, our lineage begins with you and soil and breath. The soil from which we came is lost to us, but you are Ground of our being. Grow in us fruit of joy and resistance. Connect us to those from whose wombs and loins we emerged. Connect us all the way back to the first mother and the first father." G-d is entangled with ancestors because G-d is the first ancestor. G-d is the mysterious Mother-Father who birthed us all. Our prayers were petitions to know ourselves. Our prayers were entreaties for G-d not to leave us storyless.

* * *

The story we hear about this place we call these United States excludes my story and the rich stories of so many others. And now, to block our stories by law, states and localities are banning the telling of the true stories of us. The enemies of love and freedom have always known the power of stories. They make up stories to control us and to increase their power. They sprinkle the spice of exceptionalism over the excrement of colonialism. They are trying to stop our ancestors from aiding G-d in awakening us! They are trying to make us storyless and manipulating the masses with failing attempts to set forth new ways for us to be human together.

Gladys B. Austin, my maternal grandmother, was a charmer of children. She loved them dearly and disciplined them with a steady hand. I watched her with my younger siblings. I watched her with her own great-grandchildren. She lit up in the presence of children and they lit up around her. In 1993, she and I drove to visit her infant great-grandson in Coastal Georgia. Now both my grandmother and her great-grandson are ancestors.

My 1984 Chevrolet Cavalier was not going to get us there quickly, so we talked and laughed as the miles came and went. We stopped at the Waffle House to eat. What she wanted was not on the menu, but they catered to her graciously because of her status as an elder. As we rode together, I would steal glances at her along I-16 and I-75. We were separated in age by sixty-four years, but I painstakingly cataloged every memory.

Finally, we arrived at the home of my cousin and his young bride. There is nothing like the relief when a long journey is over. The couple brought the baby over to her. And she did what she always did. She did what she did with me, my siblings, and our mother. She did what she did when she encountered infants before she ever had a child of her own.

She stood the child on her frail thighs, lifted his arms and sang:

Dance, dance lil' toh-tee, toh-tee!
Dance, dance, lil' toh-tee dance!
Dance, dance lil' toh-tee, toh-tee!
Dance, dance lil' toh-tee dance!

It never failed. My little cousin moved his feet furiously and joyfully, and we all laughed together. That song is undefeated. No child can resist its rhythm. No child could resist her smile, her spirit, her ancestral power.

I don't think she made that song up. She danced to it as an infant in 1909. And the one who sang it to her, her mother Nancy, whom she did not remember, danced to it. I heard my mother sing this song to her grandchildren. She stood them on her thighs and lifted their hands and they commenced to cut a rug.

Yes, a lot of stuff is swirling about us and around us and shadow ancestors and those who call on them are working overtime to stop us. But listen deeply, hear Mystery's song. Fall into joy. Remain human. Those of us whose arms have been lifted by ancestors cannot stop dancing. Mystery's music is undefeated.

7

Ancestral Rendezvous

I AM VERY big and very Black. My presence implicates. It stirs up ancestral angst in those committed to America as it is. My thinking and words remove all doubt as to where I stand and whom I represent. We come not to lacerate for laceration's sake. We do not believe in flagellation. And why receive truth as a beating? Why receive history as flogging? We come so that the surgery necessary to remove the cancer can begin. No cancer patient has ever survived who would not hear their diagnosis. We want healing together—for all of us. But those who deny cancer embrace death. Always and everywhere.

I turn to one of the empire's own to make the case. Samuel P. Huntington emerged from imperial central casting. He was educated at Yale, Chicago, and Harvard. He ascended the heights of the foreign affairs professoriate. He began teaching at Harvard at the age of twenty-three. Huntington coached the apartheid regime of South Africa that police violence and torture could be necessary to effect reform as he did not advocate the outright elimination of their inhumane system toward non-whites. For those who believe that Democrats are the font of domestic and global justice:

be forewarned, Huntington was a card-carrying member of that political party and served on President Jimmy Carter's National Security Council.

In *The Clash of Civilizations and the Remaking of World Order*, Samuel P. Huntington spoke truth when he said, "The West won the world not by the superiority of its ideas or values or religion . . . but rather by its superiority in applying organized violence. Westerners often forget this fact; non-Westerners never do." Those who will not hear my ancestors nor me, listen to your own.

Climbing up and out is the only option. Jesus led Peter, James, and John up a high mountain, as told by two gospels. Jesus's ascent, and ours, is not religious activity to be cordoned off and locked up in churches, bibles, and sermons about G-d's glory. This is human activity that is divine and divine activity that is human. Climbing is as political as it is religious. Those who would separate religion and politics cannot be trusted. Religion speaks to our ultimate concern and politics must be shaped by this concern—or it is farce. There has never been a separation of church and state in America's ethics. America's church has always stamped its imprimatur on America's politics. The church of my ancestors and many other traditions did not.

Those who claim that politics has no place in the church know that their politics are at loggerheads with Jesus's revolutionary gospel. What I believe, preach, and pray are profoundly political because G-d's reign rearranges every facet of human life. No part of our existence goes untouched by G-d's radical identification with humanity and G-d's will that all live as children of the Holy One.

This is the climb before us, to integrate the physical and spiritual. To claim the human body, every human body, as G-d's residence and playground. To exert ourselves in sweating our way onto new terrifying and terrific terrain. Jesus, the integrated one, led three disciples up a high mountain. High.

This is a climb worth taking. A climb that fuses the sweat of our brows with the deep yearnings of our souls. A climb that will not leave bodies at the base of the mountain, as much American religion does, and refuses to separate flesh from spirit. Through ascent we discover ancestors are indeed divine coconspirators as we climb. I am invested in ascent because the ancestors rooted me in mystery, and I know that something more is calling me. I am not sure where I am called to go. I do know that I am not called to stay here, at the foot of the mountain. None of us are called to stay here.

* * *

In 1997, I made my first international journey to Egypt, Syria, Jordan, Greece, and Israel. We landed in Damascus, where I was accosted by the following ubiquitous American exports: McDonald's, Coca-Cola, and Kentucky Fried Chicken. I also heard hip-hop music. That caused my smile to widen and my head to bob. Beautiful little brown children greeted me shouting, "Michael Jordan! Michael Jordan!" They would sing a song to me as I walked through villages and markets, "Abu Samara

Sukhara!" I was told that I was being serenaded as the "sweet Black man." Damn sure different than the songs I hear at home.

We spent a lovely evening in Egypt preparing to ride camels up Mount Sinai and watch the sun rise from that storied vista. It may have been two or three o'clock in the morning. I mounted my camel along with a fellow traveler. Our comrades moved slowly ahead of us and began to ascend. Our camels danced a little to the left and a little to the right, made a painful noise, and threw us off their backs. They refused to carry the two Americans whose weight hovered at or over the 260-pound mark for three or four hours. The camels knew the cost of climbing with added weight. The two of us stayed on the ground. Our companions ascended and returned with new stories and new songs. They found us where they had left us.

Those who go up come down differently. Those weighed down don't make it very far.

Where are you taking us, Jesus? And why? Something lies at the summit of that mountain, but not without our climbing and not without the intentional loss of the weight that keeps us back—the weight of orthodoxy, of national identity, of narratives that anchor and define us. Jesus may be taking us up because he knows that without our having seen the summit, we will not embrace our destinies upon return. We must see and hear what must be seen and heard on the mountain's peak.

The world as we know it cannot survive much longer without our making a sweaty climb up a different mountain.

We must follow ancestors unknown, or ancestors willfully silenced by the violent who hoard the power they avariciously accumulated to head in a new direction.

Once I was consumed by a naive hope. I encountered many like me. We believed that electing Black people to office would change things. We believed that keeping Democrats in power would change things. We believed that church attendance, praying, and preaching would change things. Coming to terms with the stubbornness of the systems of this world breaks bodies and spirits. Nihilism is not an option. Neither is naivete.

I have had to become honest about what hope means for people formed in traditions like my own.

I know what theologians I do not trust say about hope. I know what theologians I admire say. The truth is that people in communities of faith like my own experience and enact hope as waiting for G-d to do something. People have been so theologically malnourished as to push back when human agency, responsibility, and partnership with G-d are introduced. We cannot wait on G-d to change things any more than G-d can wait on us.

G-d made G-d's move toward us in the incarnation. It is our turn to move toward G-d and to confront the forces of death Jesus confronted in the gospels. Those forces find their fiercest articulation in the church and the state, in organized religion and imperial power. The collusion of these powers lynched Jesus.

We cannot hope that those who follow shadow ancestors and shadow systems will change, especially if hope means waiting for G-d to change them. We must be willing to sweat for change. Professor of constructive theology and African American religion Anthony Pinn has helped me by sharing a new grammar for the struggle ahead. Pinn deftly and correctly calls the traditional Christian language of hope to task in a conversation he had with Brad Braxton. Hope in our culturally Christian context requires no mountain climbing, no perspiration, and no exertion. Pinn prefers the language of *perpetual rebellion against the forces of death*. What Pinn offers is the language of perseverance. These words summon ongoing human effort in raging against the machinations of oppression and injustice.

Our struggle cannot be outcome driven, Pinn also says. We must make peace with the fact that the war against these forces will never cease. It has not stopped, nor will it. We live in an era where legislative, jurisprudential, and economic gains have been thwarted, defeated, and rolled back. Many have acted as if victories for justice would be permanent because they were morally right. This is not so. It never will be. The fight will not stop, even if there are victories. We need language that will not obfuscate this truth. Hope, I'm afraid, may not be able to carry this freight.

The text in Revelation that describes war breaking out in heaven speaks to this reality. There is no place where these shadow powers do not angle for more. Even proximity to G-d's throne does not stop them. They fight, kill, eat, and gorge themselves. We are suffering from their insatiable hunger now. That insatiable hunger must be met by our insatiable desire for Mystery to reveal in our hour what those who are motivated by being human together must know. We must fight and lament and rage while holding tightly to joy. We must hold on to joy like parents hold on to their children amid raging storms. We must hold on to joy and sing and love our way into taking our next steps up the mountain before us.

Then we rest, breathe, and climb some more.

Our efforts will be met with Divine sustenance and the wind of the Spirit. We will discover that Jesus climbs with us. His back is as drenched as ours.

What was the height of that mountain? We are left to speculate. What we do know is this: Jesus leads his students up mountains. Exertion. Perspiration. Damp backs, fatigued calves, weary thighs, and exhausted arms. This is discipleship.

Did Peter, James, and John have agency? Had Jesus cajoled, guilted, or commanded that they ascend this mountain? Couldn't they have said no to the teacher? They clearly did not always follow him as directed. We most certainly do not have this practice of saying no in polite, bourgeois American Christianity. In this version of Christianity, Jesus does not summon us to climb mountains. Our faith is largely fixed on our comfort and self-actualization. We reach our potential, we discover that we are champions (of what, exactly?), we maximize our marriages and relationships. These things are important. But, friend, where is the mountain climbing?

Jesus takes three of his friends with him. Two of the gospel writers say they journeyed up the mountain by themselves. No other disciples joined them. But the four ascended together. Ascent here does not happen alone. The Human One takes sometimes faithful, sometimes faltering folk with him. This is not a whosoever will. The phrase "by themselves" keeps us from including the usual crowds of women and men who followed Jesus. And I am not convinced that this climb happened only once. Seems to me that Jesus needed numerous encounters such as this one to stay the course. Climbing alone, I would have turned back often without experiencing what awaited them at the summit. I am sure that Jesus would have turned back, too.

Only the kind of rendezvous that awaited this small band can keep us climbing. And these rendezvous cannot happen once. We must return to these places of liminal space and ancestor luminosity to remain richly human and sensitive to the divinity coursing through our lungs and lymph nodes with every breath we take on the mountain. *Spirit* means simply breath or wind. Spiritual awareness is bodily awareness, is breath awareness. It is embracing the Afro-Asiatic poetry of scripture in Genesis and of James Weldon Johnson in "The Creation." We exist because we are temporary recipients of Divine breath on this plane.

Human beings are breath borrowers. When Breath leaves us, we are no more. The spiritual life calls us to an unfailing awareness of Breath in ourselves and others. When we live in the fullness of this glorious truth, that all bodies are holy because they are Breath-filled, we are compelled to love extravagantly and to fight valiantly against those who would keep us from breathing.

It cannot be lost on us that climbing requires more breath and more Breath. Physiological demands and spiritual ones are wed as Jesus and his friends stay the course. It is no different for any of us. Simultaneously, our lungs will demand more oxygen to nourish our bodies, and our inner selves will demand more Breath to sustain our souls.

One gospel writer says they went up the mountain to pray. If prayer were a school, I would have been suspended or expelled long ago. Prayer, beyond perfunctory religious stuff, has been my aim for many years. More than saying grace before meals, more than liturgical prayer in worship, more than asking for stuff or for forgiveness, I have wanted to learn to pray—I mean, *really pray*.

But I have been stubborn, lazy, and unrealistic about prayer. I was unwilling to get as vulnerable with G-d as I felt that G-d was with me. Prayer can't happen without mutual self-disclosure. I was too busy protecting myself and wrapping my nakedness and pain. In that scenario, Spirit has little with which to work.

I didn't want prayer to be work. I wasn't willing to sweat, climb, or exert significant energy. I refused to show up day after day with the discipline and determination necessary for depth of relationship. I wanted to dive but I never abandoned the shallow end of the pool.

I was a graduate of America's school of capitalist, acquisitive prayer. I prayed to control teenage angst, lust, and desire. I prayed for better grades. I prayed to not get caught by my parents or others in authority. Prayer was not a deep longing for G-d or a deep yearning for awareness or truth. Prayer was transactional.

The Black church has a rich tradition of gratitude in prayer. I practiced that. But after gratitude, prayer was getting G-d to do stuff for me or others that we could not do for ourselves. It was not all selfish. But it always felt transactional. Gratitude became the pretext for my barrage of requests. Even intercessory prayer fit this mold.: "Thank you, God. Help me. Fix me. Give me. Help them. Fix them. Give them. Forgive me. Forgive us. In Jesus's name. Amen." Not about G-d. All about us.

Great teachers helped me to expand my thinking about prayer and my being then expanded by prayer. Prayer is awareness of G-d. It is living each second with the knowledge that G-d is with us, and we are caught up in the Divine life. We are never alone. We climb together.

Prayer alters vision and perception. Prayer gives us eyes to see G-d in every human, plant, animal, and circumstance—good or bad. Ancestral teachers illuminate prayer, ensuring the prayer drenched person sees in themselves and the world what others cannot.

We use words all the time. But words can be absolutely useless in prayer. Prayer can fill the heart with knowledge too wonderful for words. In silence, prayer communicates and accomplishes more than speech ever could.

Prayer is opening a door through which G-d can enter. Prayer is extending a hand that G-d can grasp. Prayer is conversation. In prayer, I wait for G-d to speak. Or, I slow down enough to hear what G-d has been saying all along.

Jesus and his friends didn't go up the mountain to clasp their hands and throw words at G-d. They went to open themselves to desire. This is risky and potentially painful for G-d and for us. Even so, G-d desired to be in relationship with them and they desired to be in relationship with G-d. Their prayers consisted of wordless waiting and awareness of G-d's presence. They came to Breath out of breath. And they breathed. They ascended to Light. And they radiated.

There is a tradition that tells us prayer, being saturated with G-d's very being, causes physical transformation. Moses's face shone brightly in Exodus 34 after he had spoken with G-d. He was unaware of his radiant countenance. It struck fear in the hearts of those around him such that they would not come near Moses. When Moses went in to commune with G-d he took his veil off. When he returned among the people, he veiled his face. Prayer is the space where nothing separates G-d from us, and nothing separates us from G-d. Moses withheld nothing and was filled by Presence that lighted his body in a way that all could see.

The closest I ever came to a transformative prayer discipline was when I was in seminary, oddly enough. Seminarians are normally too busy reading, writing, and stressing to give much thought to prayer. I was convicted in my dorm room one day. I knew that if I did not come to a more intimate knowledge of G-d all would be for naught. I would leave Duke with student loans and a life sentence of talking about a G-d I didn't truly know. I had seen too many preacher/prisoners. I didn't want to be one.

I decided to purchase yet another devotional book. Every morning for a month I spent time with it I made myself do it. Especially when it was the last thing I wanted to do. And in that month, I learned to truly be present. By the end of the month, I felt different.

That semester I was interning at a United Methodist Church. My supervisor noticed something. "Bill," he said, "What is going on with you? You aren't the same." I knew exactly what he meant. But said I didn't. And changed the subject quickly. His question jarred me. Shortly thereafter I stopped that morning practice. For years I have asked myself why. And for years my answer was that I did not want to share control with G-d. And my answer now is that often I do not want to share myself with G-d.

The dedicated work of ascent of the four meant that Jesus, and possibly his companions, were beyond protecting themselves from G-d. They made themselves available to the radical freedom and self-giving, other-affirming love that marks the divine life.

Then Jesus suddenly experienced a radical physical change. Each gospel writer reports what occurred differently.

Mark says Jesus was transfigured before them and his clothes became dazzling bright such as no one on earth could brighten them. Matthew reports that Jesus's face shone like the sun and his clothes became bright as light. Luke observes that Jesus's face changed, and his clothes became as bright as a flash of lightening. The Mosaic tradition informs their telling. But with Jesus, not only is his physical countenance changed but also all that touches him is set ablaze in light. His metamorphosis causes all matter in contact with him to be metamorphosed as well. Even his clothing is transformed.

Exegetes I have consulted spend most of their interpretive energies on Jesus's stunning transformation in the presence of his friends. That is a worthy pursuit. They spend quite a bit of time on his clothing as well. Interesting reading, no doubt. But what is it that these interpreters do not, cannot, or refuse to see?

Here in the synoptic gospels, gleaming like Jesus's face and his clothing, is an ancestral visitation.

Suddenly Moses and Elijah appear. They are not described as spirits, phantoms, or apparitions. Luke calls them two men. Men. And they were talking with Jesus. Those who claim scripture's inerrancy and infallibility, those who read the text literally, what say you? What do you do with this text? It has been here all along, but my—our eyes—were trained not to see this for what it is.

I am not a biblical literalist. I reject the doctrines of inerrancy and infallibility. Too often they are used to bludgeon people into belief while not escorting them into the beautiful possibilities that await those who know that G-d is among us as one of us. I am more dangerous than defenders of infallibility and inerrancy. I take the text *seriously* as a G-d–breathed, Spirit orchestrated human creation.

The bible, that library of books offering multiple perspectives on divinity and humanity and so much more, is both blessed and bedeviled. It is not basic instructions before leaving earth. It is complex, containing many literary genres and no singular moral or ethical code. The bible is no holy Magic 8 Ball. It can't be shaken up or turned to a random page where it will answer all our questions and solve all our problems.

Within this mountain text that tells us many things, of key importance is this: The early church was not averse to nor ashamed of ancestral visitation and conversation. Moses and Elijah not only appear in physical, visual form. They talk with Jesus.

My favorite preachers have the capacity to imagine what the text excludes. My rabbinical colleagues teach that we must read under, over, and between the words of the text. What did the lawgiver say to the Human One? What words came from the mouth of the prophet?

Tradition comes alive at mountain's peak. Time intersects with eternity. Life brushes up against death. Kairos kisses Chronos. All this and more happens when ancestors appear and speak. If Jesus, who was as present with G-d as a human could be, was gifted with ancestral visitation and conversation, how much more do we need the same? There are places we cannot go without climbing mountains and reaching apexes together. The ancestors await us at the summit. And there our summit, our ancestral dialogue, begins.

Scripture only hints toward what was shared between Jesus, Moses, and Elijah. Luke says they discussed Jesus's exodus, his departure. Ancestral work prepares us for what is to come. They walked the paths we trod. They know the roads before us. Ancestors cannot take our steps for us, but they can light our path. They could light the grueling path that was set before Jesus, that path of radical, costly faithfulness to G-d. Both Moses and Elijah knew the cost of such faithfulness. Their insight and energy and words, did they make the difference for Jesus in those exodus days?

Only once do we read of this kind of visitation in the gospels. Yet, I am convinced this event pointed to others. It is not a discrete incident. As I said, Jesus would have needed this kind of nourishment often. For the work ahead of us, we will, too. Visitations and conversations like these can keep us going even in storms of opposition and doubt.

My paternal grandmother visited me in a dream. She was wearing that green, checkered house dress. We sat at the Formica kitchen table in my great-grandparents' home, something we never did while she was with us. We talked and laughed. She spoke to me, advising me to stay the course, to write the book. I found every reason not to put pen to paper, finger to key. I was seized by something beyond lethargy and procrastination. I was frozen. Thawing spiritually and intellectually seemed an impossibility.

She told me who I was. She showed me who I was. I saw images of my great-grandfather working as a blacksmith. I saw my maternal grandmother making bricks of beauty without straw. Through her I was plunged into family gatherings of old where there was laughter and hope. Without words, I was being told that I had something to offer that was in me, but not only of me. I had to make good on the ancestral deposit within. She gave me terra firma. I placed my feet on this solid foundation. I moved slowly, then confidently. She came to tell me who I was.

Moses and Elijah appear to Jesus and talk with him. This scene is happening in the synoptic gospels near the time Jesus shares the cost of following him. Faith demands sweat. Faith helps us keep moving toward the ancestors who meet us atop our mountains of exhaustion and exhilaration. There Jesus, his friends, and the ancestors hear the Voice saying, "This is my son. He is chosen. He is beloved. Listen to him."

Ancestors connect us to Voice, so we can hear more clearly our names and our destinies as they guide us and lead us. Surrounded by a great cloud of witnesses we must listen. From that same cloud, Voice speaks. We share time and space with ancestors whenever Voice speaks. If we hold to this epiphany, through good and bad times, when we leave the mountain, we will never be the same.

8

Ancestral Design

AFTER SUCCESSFULLY COMPLETING my coursework for a graduate degree in African American preaching and sacred rhetoric, I was struggling to complete my comprehensive examinations, taking forever to schedule the exams. Intimidation seized me. I would have to demonstrate to my formidable professors that I was aware of scholarship's past and present discussions in the fields of rhetoric and homiletics. I also had dissertation-specific questions on theologies of the cross and African theological rhetoric.

Exams were held on four consecutive Mondays, beginning at 8:00 a.m. and to be completed by 5:00 p.m. Every week for a month I was walking the plank. My brain and my insides were seized, frozen. My program director sent me an email, I experienced as a thinly veiled threat: "Bill Lamar, you must complete these exams by March 1." That's how it happens for me. Big thing before me. Due dates and deadlines hurtling my way. Back against the wall. Frozen.

I was not about to allow the arduous coursework I had completed to go up in flames of fear or the molasses of procrastination. I had to get over myself. I had to get the work done. I had to complete this degree.

This is not just my story. It may be yours or the story of someone you cherish. Yes, my calling to study Black preaching has been clear. The beauty, poetry, complexity, and diversity of this art form has stretched me and saved me. The majesty of Black theologians, preachers, and teachers enlivens me. Wiliam Augustus Jones moves me. The richness of Renita Weems nourishes me. The power of Prathia Hall emboldens me. The artistry of Gardner Calvin Taylor soul-stirs me. This is the homiletic tradition that I probe, that I want to learn how it functions rhetorically and theologically.

I knew I was called to this work because I was equally thrilled and frightened at the prospect. Calling for me has never unfolded like a rom-com, where the two lovers finally sprint across the airport and embrace one another. It has been more like an album containing greatest hits and greatest misses. Calling has sometimes been ecstasy because I know what I am doing and why I am doing it. Calling has sometimes been drudgery because the work is daunting and draining and I can't tune my mind and body to the frequency of the deepest desire: That desire to be who the Divine and the ancestors are calling me to be.

Maybe you feel the same way. Deeply called to some significant work in the world. Compelled to use your spiritual and intellectual resources to make this world better. You want to give your body, your energy, your life force to an idea, an organization, a community, a people, a purpose. As my ancestors would say, you know this "as sure as you're born."

This thing gnawing at you and nagging you and inspiring you is as real as the beautiful, fragile gift of life that you possess and that possesses you. Think for a moment about that call or those callings that you embrace and avoid. Rest in that vocational gravitational pull that powerfully attracts you and the trepidation that potently repels you. Because callings are nothing if not costly. To be changed ourselves and to change our world we must sit in this tension, learn from it, and harness its positive and negative energies to go forward.

There are organizations to start and transform. There are books and songs to write. There are institutions to rejuvenate. There are gifts to be shared. I know that there are things that persistently arrest your attention and invite your intentions.

But there is also just some shit that will not leave us alone! That keeps us frozen. What is it for you? Feel that. Listen to that. Love that. Leave that. Come back to that. And love it all over again.

In order to lean into that which I must do yet assiduously avoid, that which I want to accomplish with all my heart, yet am loathe to begin, I have to design space. That is hilarious for me to write. I am the most non-architect, non-artist, non-engineer in the world. But I must *design* space. It is hard for me to think spatially and three-dimensionally, but I have to design space. You have to design space, too. And first, we must design internal space.

I had to design internal space to get my work done. A better way to write about this is, that I had to design internal space to let the work *come*. This is not trickery or magic. The work still demands discipline, effort, and focus. But when the call is upon you, and the world wants what is inside of you to be born, Spirit will be your midwife. I sense Spirit most keenly when I prepare a space for Spirit to alight, like a butterfly on a bright flower. Spirit is always present, but my awareness is heightened when I have designed my heart to be attuned.

My best space is when the work comes because I am open and ready. Often this heady openness and readiness is seasoned with heaping tablespoons of pressure, too. But internal space is always key. Freeing myself of soul clutter and spirit baggage allows me to welcome that which has wanted to come for a long time.

Inside of us are voices saying that this work of finishing my degree or your work of changing your community will be hard. Possibly too hard to start and even harder to finish. When those voices arise in me, so do ancestral voices. Ancestral voices say, "We have done hard before." There are also shadow ancestor voices saying, "Why do this? This kind of effort is not necessary. You will still eat and pay your bills and go on vacation if you don't do this." And other ancestral voices will counter, asking, "Since when are we only concerned with food, money, and leisure?"

There are voices that tell us we are okay where we are. Okay doing no more than what we are already doing. I differentiate the voices. My internal voice keeps speaking in the first person. But Ancestral voices scream *we* are not okay! They speak, employing plural, communal language. The ancestors kept pulling me toward a purposeful *we* that doesn't erase my fingerprints but summons me to be awakened to the knowledge that my hand was in the hands of those who had come before me and those who were to come.

Still, I would listen to my own excuses. Still, I would be weighed down Erykah Badu–style by my baggage. Yet, the unrelenting ancestral voices called me by name. I had trained myself to let internal voices of doubt and discouragement control the volume of the sounds of my soul. I now know that I can authorize ancestral voices to command my sacred soundscape so that I will move in the world to the music of the extraordinary, the sublime, the otherwise impossible. With their help, I design my internal space. So must you.

I also had to design external space. To prepare for torturous exams required design. To preach Sunday after Sunday demands design. To do the work of organizing for justice requires design. To write this book demands design. For you to prepare lesson plans, perform surgery, close deals, prepare meals, and care for elders and children requires that you design space that feeds your soul. I could not sit down at our kitchen table and write without the right design. Disquieted within myself, I asked, was this a Bill Lamar procrastination tactic? No, it was not. Clear direction emerged. I would not finish these exams without the right design.

Dana, my gift of a wife, had successfully walked the comprehensive exam journey before me. Her sisters mailed her a card nearly thirty years ago to encourage her to finish the good work she had begun. The card, faded a bit, still carries that loving energy. Now it carries loving energy intensified over time. Right before I wrote my first exam, Dana put that card on the kitchen table. It was a chilly Monday morning, but my heart was as warm as the tea that filled the Metropolitan African Methodist Episcopal Church mug that rested by my side. The design I needed was taking shape. But something was still missing.

And then it came to me. My mother had given me Aunt Viney's picture in the oval frame. During Christmas in Tallahassee with my family, I took that picture to a photo shop. I had 3 × 5 and 5 × 7 prints made, gifts for my brother Marty and my sister Kerri. I kept a 3 × 5 for myself.

I set that photo of Aunt Viney next to the card. The right design. I was ready to write.

Aunt Viney's picture had watched me as a child. She seemed eerily trapped in that photograph yet strangely liberated from the strictures of space and time. I needed her in my space at that time. She had saved my grandmother. She saved us. Her handsome face saw me, although she had never seen me at my kitchen table, doing difficult work. Something I had to do. Something I didn't want to do. Something I wanted to do. I kept writing. Four Mondays came. Kitchen table, card, warm mug, Aunt Vinny's photo. Keys clickety clacking.

Four Mondays went. I turned in my exams. I got them back from my formidable professors. I completed my comprehensives with commendations. Designing the space made a difference for me. Ancestral design rooted me and pushed me forward.

We all design ancestrally. We may not call it that. That's fine. Call it what you will or call it nothing at all. It is in us. We hang portraits. We cherish jewelry, clothing, furniture, and artifacts from those who have ascended. This connects us. This reminds us that we are not alone. It subtly makes us aware of the sacrifices that power our lives.

A picture of the house my father's family rented in East Macon prior to urban renewal—*Negro removal* as the elders called it—hangs in my parent's home. My grandparents would give my daddy the house rent to take to Reverend Benford, the rentier. No telephone in the house. Baths were taken in a tin tub on the porch. My niece and nephew have heard this story time and again. They must hear it. Daddy insists that they know that their great-grandfather labored for meager wages in a textile mill and their great-grandmother washed white folks' clothes to fill that little rented home with love and protection during a time when no love or protection were afforded them outside of the caring conclave of their color.

Daddy putting this picture on the wall is ancestral design. A refusal to forget. An honoring of sweat long evaporated and tears long dried. An homage to laughter still echoing beyond the veil.

Another ancestral community design has been this: our porches. Black people love porches. Just about everybody had one. Some were small. Some were big. All were necessary. It gets as hot as Hades in Georgia in the summer. And the porch was where we cooled in the evening when the sun was at rest. We would sit outside with the elders, and they would greet everyone who passed. It was pure joy.

My parents designed and built a screened porch onto their home. Just like the ancestors before us, we sat there and laughed and talked, ate and cried. One Christmas day, Daddy and I were sitting. Just the two of us. The porch spirit was thick as molasses, and memories came rushing in. I heard a story I had never heard before. Daddy recounted getting a bike for Christmas as a child. He cried and said that it was a used bike that his father had gussied up for his baby boy, his last son he called "Lil' Un." And in his story I now knew that the slick, red, brand spanking new Western Flyer bike I got for Christmas in 1982 was something much, much more. We cried together. Not sure if that would have ever happened except on the porch. That is by *design*.

The work of design, the ancestrally designed spaces where you live, work, and play—this is work done thoughtfully and lovingly. Design is meant to connect us with the best traditions of our past. I envision people like us helping communities, governments, houses of worship and places of business to design in such a way that the best communitarian impulses soak deeply into our bones through art, statuary, architecture, and artifacts. Ancestral design will be guru, and we will be students. Ancestral design will be griot, and we will be rapt audience. And the dead—the living dead—will walk among us and tell us stories of resurrection.

Unless we privilege the life forces of the unborn and the dead, we will remain adrift, unmoored. Our sociopolitical and economic decisions must privilege those who have not yet made their appearances. We are being crushed under the weight of those whose commitment is only to themselves and their brief lifetimes. They build systems to serve themselves. They worship at the altar of their lust for power and control.

We must design a world spiritually, aesthetically, and politically that asks, "What of our children to the seventh generation?" and "What is the path of our human-loving (philanthropic) ancestors?" We ask these questions for a design that will save us. If we keep rejecting these questions, we will foreclose on the possibility of tomorrow. Ancestral design is not frivolity. It is fundamental to our survival.

Why did Martin Luther King Jr. keep a portrait of Gandhi in his home? Why did Howard Washington Thurman keep a portrait of his grandmother, Nancy Ambrose, in his study? Why did Nanny keep Aunt Viney's image in the place of prominence? Yes, they wanted to remember. But they also wanted to be shaped into people imbued with the spirits of those whose images they privileged. That shaping is accomplished over time with tools wielded by the ancestors and powered by their ongoing energy among us.

Mama Itihari Touré reminds those of us who study under her tutelage that in many African traditions, objects have personhood. They are not just wood, plastic, or paper. They have energy. They have being. They have power. Many steeped in Western ways of knowing are offended by this. They would call this idea pagan, animist, anti-Christian or some other ignorant, pejorative term. But damage the precious items, portraits, or places of those people who decry that energy of ancestral objects and you discover their truth: They will rage, they will act viscerally and violently. Don't pay attention to the beliefs they claim to hold. Believe their actions alone to speak the truth.

We all know deep in our bones that objects are more than things. They carry us back. They push us forward.

Be clear, though, designing ancestral space is not a cocreation in the interest of capitalist notions of productivity. This is not our intent. Yes, internal and external ancestral design helped me accomplish a big and important task. (And I need that design to help me to keep pressing forward.) But it was not just about getting exams written. And it is not just about crossing the next huge project off an ever-expanding to-do list. Ancestral design helps intention to be set and allows space to assist in midwifing that which desires to spring forth from us. The things that wish to be born in and through us need assistance, by ancestral design.

The ways of being human together that want to manifest among us are like new life. New life is always fragile. Midwives know that new life requires embracing every possibility for survival. The creativity that wants to emerge from us all, not just some special class of artists or writers or scholars, requires ancestral design, encouragement, and wisdom. When we languish in our work in the world, and fatigue and self-doubt seize us, connect with that innumerable caravan, that great cloud of witnesses. They will cheer and demand you toward completion, which is nothing other than the full embrace of yourself, the ancestors, and the gifts you came to offer the world.

How is your space designed? Whose portraits hang on the walls of your home, office, church, synagogue, mosque, or sacred gathering space? Each portrait is an attempt for the living to commune with the living dead. And though we may not be paying attention to these images, they still set intention and communicate loudly. Those who hung these images did so to clearly mark space for the living and those yet to come. The ancestors of these images pay attention to us, helping us design space.

When I lead people on tours of Metropolitan African Methodist Episcopal Church, I allow the architecture and the portraiture to tell stories too deep for words. We are story-craving beings before we are storytellers. And the best storyteller is silence wrapped in awe and unknowing. This is where imagination thrives. This is by design. I try not to get in the way.

At our church, Metropolitan, we gather in the Bishop Robert Lee Pruitt Boardroom to meet, study, pray, and fellowship. The room is filled with stately photographs matted in purple and framed in rich, dark woods. The space evokes reverence. When people enter, they lower their voices and their eyes meet the eyes of servants of our denomination, some long asleep, some recently deceased, a few still among us. They behold men who achieved beyond the constraints of bondage. And they behold women who soared beyond boundaries set for them in our patriarchal and too often misogynoir system.

These pictures demand our questions: Who were these people? Why so many men and so precious few women? And the pictures also ask questions. Who are you that look upon us? What are you doing with your precious life? They speak: We once walked and stumbled and breathed like you. Now we are no longer in your realm. You are on your way to ours.

The Pruitt Boardroom is beneath our sanctuary. Our community of faith rests upon the energies, stories, triumphs, failures, and challenges of those whose images adorn that room and countless others whose names and images are lost to us but held intimately by the Divine. And as I look at the images in the boardroom, they always seem to be asking me, "What can we do together?"

Metropolitan African Methodist Episcopal Church stands sentinel over the capital of the American empire. It is my ground zero in a city that is a case study in ancestral design. Design and power go hand in hand. Those using shadow power to design are storytellers who often privilege one story over many stories. They also erase stories. Erasing the stories of people is a violent act that portends greater violence to come. Rampant today, story-erasers become those who exploit, oppress, and eliminate the people whose stories they expunge. They, their shadow ancestors, and their progeny will methodically follow this same pattern of escalation and death.

The designers of America's imperial capital did not design space in the interest of furthering dialogue or gathering voices and people together. They designed to magnify the narrative of the victor while suppressing how the victory was won. What kind of place would this be if other voices were given space? What kind of place would this be if other names were named and other images remembered? Images of Indigenous peoples whose land was pillaged and plundered. The Africans whose labor was stolen. And I do not mean that we need a statue here and a school named for a lover of liberty there. I mean that we need a complete redesign and overhaul of the spiritual, physical, political, and emotional space that we share.

We who are children of violently erased stories carry the memory of those untold chronicles in our blood and bones. We know that we were present building, laughing, loving, falling, failing, and rising again. We hear whispers from beyond that verify these truths. The seen world does not match the universe's humming and screaming inside of us. The unseen worlds in us demand to be made manifest. A manifestation that doesn't eliminate others or violently suppress them, but one to make all stories part of humanity's symphony.

The unseen world demands that the seen world manifest certain realities. There cannot be rest personally nor politically when the unseen world is consistently denied, silenced, or ignored. What we continue to experience in this place called the United States are attempts to silence the screams of the unseen world, the world of wind, breath, and spirit. Mendaciously designed space and rhetoric that dresses the violence of empire in garments of liberty are employed to quiet us. This strategy is hollow and insulting. The unseen world keeps birthing those who question, fight, organize, write, sing, dance and design space who are not deterred by those who seek to mute our stories.

What is seen is created by the unseen. This is the Genesis creation story. This the substance of the creation stories of so many cultures. The unseen is still creating. We are our best selves when we do not fight what the unseen is trying to create. That creation is beautiful and just and abundant for all, without exception.

The goal of humanity is to live in harmony with the unseen, the heavens, the Divine. This is central to the Africana philosophy of Ma'at according to scholar Maulana Karenga. As above, so below. The seen manifesting the unseen. The Christian scriptures put it this way: What is bound on earth is bound in heaven. What is loosed on earth is loosed in heaven (Matthew 16:19). The seen and the unseen are beautifully, frustratingly, and inextricably bound. We must design in a way that what is seen is a portal to that which we cannot see; that which calls us to love of self, others, creation, and the Divine. Ancestral design is the unseen world asserting itself in the seen world. It is power brought forth, light cast, a way made. It is choosing life for us all.

There are also unseen voices calling us toward destruction. The geopolitics, economics, and theologies of our day can only be partially explained by scholarship, journalism, and punditry. Western ways of knowing pretend to make little room for the power of the unseen world, yet what we see is powered by shadow forces that are ancestral and potent. Those who refuse to create a world of shared abundance and human flourishing stir ancestral pots frequently and to great effect. They call forth the energies of those who were misanthropic in life. Some seek to recreate ancestors of light after their own images. They make light into shadow, and they call the night, day. We must never lose sight of this.

Ancestors of light, whose unseen voices call us to a human-honoring, planet-valuing future, push us to design internal space that will make deep listening to the wisdom of the ages possible and delightful. Our internal space must be open to the creative and destructive winds of Spirit, which build up that which is just and beautiful and tear down that which is unjust and unlovely. Our internal terrain must flourish with a diverse ecosystem of rivers of peace, meadows of joy, skies of possibilities, mountains that call forth risky climbs, and valleys that make possible beautiful rest. Communion with ancestors of light can help to build rich internal worlds like these.

The places where we eat, pray, play, love, gather, and rest can become havens of harmony and outposts where our differences and disagreements can be resolved creatively and without violence. The earth rages in heat and fire because we do not value harmony with the planet that sustains us. We are literally fractious to the point of conflagration because we will not live into the harmony that is possible among us. My ancestors spoke the truth that it is possible to "study war no more." But war among ourselves and with our planet is profitable. Until life can be measured in ways not valued by American capitalism, we may be doomed, damned, or both. We must be aware of the shadow ancestral forces that make it seem impossible to choose another path. And we must be aware of the ancestral forces of light that demand that we blaze new trails and point the way.

Extraction, unrestrained commodification, and oppression are built on lies. Those who will not move from these ways of being have fooled themselves into believing that they will survive even if the planet and the rest of us die. They will extend their colonizing to Mars or the moon. They will dwell secure in fancy bunkers carved deep into the bowels of the earth.

The earth they have set aflame may consume us all in fires of greed. And then it will regenerate and creatures who dwell in harmony with it will thrive once again. Humans are not indispensable. We are but animated soil. How do we design in order to remind ourselves of our interdependence, fragility, and glory? That is the question.

* * *

Is how we design the world a feeble attempt to defy mortality? I am struck by the words we say at funerals, because I officiate them and meet families in the valley of death's ever-looming shadow. We say things at the time of death that are not true. Chief among them, are statements like this, "We will never forget you." The *we* in this well-worn statement means more than just those who knew the descendant well. *We* means the human family. And . . . we will forget. Most of us remain unknown to one another in life and in death. Stone monuments and markers are not the remedy. I have walked in many a cemetery, many a memory garden, where wind and sun and rain have erased names and dates painstakingly etched in concrete and stone.

I know where Big Daddy's mother, Panola Norman Lamar, rests. He buried her and placed a neat concrete slab above her remains. He wrote "Mother" into the concrete before it set. Big Daddy's etching was barely visible the last time I visited our family plots at Camp Hope Cemetery. Eighty years of Georgia heat, wind, rain, and chill have done their work on Grandma's memorial stone. We design to remember because we know we will forget. We say we will always remember because we know that one day we will be forgotten.

But we must remember. We must design our spaces and our gatherings together to tell the stories of who we have been and who we can become. I will not fight to be remembered. I will not rage against time nor the earth to carve my name into something I consider to be permanent no matter the cost, like the little boys carved their names into desks and trees in my youth. I will live as a story among the stories that make me possible. I will always call their names. I will tell of how I am because they are. And when I am gone my story will be enfolded into theirs. Others may choose to tell it. Regardless, I live. I seek not to differentiate myself from the flow of humanity who will sweep me into time's swift transition soon. My story ultimately will not be remembered. But where humans are joyfully living into the fullness of their divine possibilities, I will be there. So will all who came before me.

I see how we design ancestrally, for good and for ill, yet we neglect to tell the stories of the ancestors who surround us. This is an active, egregious forgetting. As a child, ancestral design appealed to me and caused me to ask many questions of my elders. Much to their chagrin, I inquired about every picture, keepsake, memorial plate, and cherished possession. Many others passed by pictures every day without being much concerned about who, what, where, or why. Now I am aware that my attention was grasped by something greater, an energy that beckoned me to draw closer and to know and be known. Ancestors were doing something in space and reaching for me to do something in time.

These flags, statues, portraits, and monuments around us demand our intense questioning: Who do they celebrate? Who do they denigrate? Are they there to speak for all of us? Are they there to summon us to be human together, or to assert the victory of one over another? We must interrogate these living objects to know the design of spaces. Yet, whether we interrogate them or not, their energy among us is real.

At some level we feel disjointed when we are surrounded by symbols we do not understand. And we feel assaulted when surrounded by symbols intended to exclude us and to tell stories of domination and power.

Metropolitan African Methodist Episcopal Church in Washington, DC, is ancestral design made flesh. I have had the privilege of welcoming people from all over the globe into our sacred space. People visit Washington from everywhere. Their curiosity takes them all over the city and many find us at 1518 M Street Northwest. Sometimes, as tourists walk toward 16th Street to stroll toward the White House, Metropolitan reaches for them, calls out to them. They approach with a fast gait. Other destinations are calling them. But their peripheral vision gifts them with an unexpected sight. Their necks crane. Their heads lift. They slow down and they look with their whole bodies. They stop, read the signs, and make their way to our front doors.

Another interesting phenomenon to observe is the busy commuters hoofing it to their workplaces, apartments, parking garages, or using various modes of transportation. They are of a different ilk than tourists. They are dressed for work, not leisure. Adorned in muted colors and dress sneakers and cradling cups of coffee and bottles of water, they walk with purpose. They are on a mission. Their name badges thump their chests rhythmically with each stride. They are on their way to scan in somewhere or to scan out. They have walked by Metropolitan one hundred times. They were always seen by Metropolitan. But they may have never returned that gaze. Finally, serendipitously, they catch a glimpse, and they slow down. Miracle of miracles. Our gorgeous structure seduces them. Their faces carry looks of calm confusion. Where did this building come from? Does it belong here?

The questions they ask of Metropolitan are born of surprise and curiosity. Where did this anachronistic architectural gem come from? *The minds and hearts of Black people.* Has it always been here? *No. It will not be here for eternity. All human creations, even those we deem holy, rise and fall. But Metropolitan is here now. Blocks away from executive imperial power. And here it will stand for many years to come.*

The ancestors who designed this space were making a grand and glorious statement. They knew that they were children of the Divine, and they created a space of welcome for all who shared their human lot. All! They designed a space of grandeur because they knew themselves to be grand and they desired that their progeny would live into their destiny. They desired a beautiful and sturdy space to sacralize human joy, mark human suffering, worship, pray, and learn. Our ancestors knew that freedom work would be unrelenting in this place.

Metropolitan is an affirmative theological and cultural statement. It does not lament exclusion in America's mainstream (read: white institutions). It gets to the business of open doors. It does not exist in the shadow of anything American. It dances in the universal, human light. Metropolitan is the work of spirit-people from around this land. Its sublime stained-glass windows tell the story of collectivity in a culture of death-dealing individualism. People from Arkansas, Alabama, Georgia, Texas, and Tennessee sent their money to build our national church in the late nineteenth century. Their largesse lives in color and light in our windows. Some who gave never saw Metropolitan, but they *saw* Metropolitan. They saw what they could construct as a force for creativity and community in the crucible of American imperial violence. Through many dangers, toils, and snares we yet stand.

How did these spirit-people, driven by Divine wind and stubborn sinew, build a place for all G-d's children? How did they determine from the outset that the house of G-d would be open to and for all? There is not one recorded incident of anyone being turned away. There is no iconography lauding the forces of death in either window or on pew. This is truly a house of prayer for all people. The impulse of its founding is truly human and truly democratic.

Not far from Metropolitan African Methodist Episcopal Church stands the Washington National Cathedral. This awe-inspiring structure is known to many because it hosts many events of national importance and lends a Christian veneer to the liturgies of American civil religion. It is the nation's church for mourning and celebration. Presidents are funeralized there. Imperial wars have been sacralized there.

Justice has been demanded there. Ensconced in the marvelous stained glass of the National Cathedral until recently was Confederate iconography and Lost Cause symbology. The Cathedral has taken these windows down in contrition and replaced them with images that would cause the death of those who installed the Confederate windows if they could see them.

The fact is that the Washington National Cathedral may be endeavoring to be a house of prayer for all people today, but that was not its founding impulse. Period. Full stop. It celebrated a mythology that enslaved benighted Africans and used poor whites as cannon fodder to keep rich, white slavocrats in power. The National Cathedral lifted that story. Metropolitan lifted the gospel story. The Confederate windows of the National Cathedral, a gift from the United Daughters of the Confederacy in 1953, were given to reassert white supremacy in a sacred space as Black people's ongoing and unbroken struggle against American empire heated up in the middle of the twentieth century.

The founders of the National Cathedral knew what the founders of Metropolitan knew. They had read the same texts. They were aware of the movement of the same Spirit that animates us all. Why was one group more morally aware? Why was one group more spiritually aware? Why was one group more human? The god of those who have made peace with oppression and exploitation is not the G-d of those who welcome all. The excellent spirits of those who built institutions like Metropolitan are the ancestral energies that can lead us forward.

The founders of so many American institutions determined that they did not have to act humanly toward those who were not like them. This same deadly moral smallness infects politics, economics, and religion today. We must make no excuses for the rank inhumanity of America's founders. We must make no excuses for those who continue in their path of exclusion and accumulation of wealth and power at all costs.

Metropolitan was designed to embody the world as it ought to be. The Washington National Cathedral was designed to sacralize America's imperial status quo. Metropolitan has not had to replace any stained glass because we did not elevate to holy status any ideology that was not founded upon justice, beauty, and truth. Not one flag is in our windows. Not even Old Glory. We knew the true nature of the nation state. And we know that America has never been as good as its promise to all its people. Our ancestors designed differently and lived differently. Those who designed the National Cathedral failed to create a space for all people and they aided and abetted a nation that did the same.

And what about you and the institutions you hold dear in designing space and intention? Do you ask, how can we design so that those who come after us will not be saddled with the onerous work of repairing the injustices we have left to fester and consume human vitality? Those who design humanly are consumed by questions such as these: Who is not seated at the table of abundance? Why aren't they there? How can we get them there?

The Akan people of Ghana's philosophy of Sankofa are indispensable in their wisdom of designing spaces of human thriving in communities. There is no way to remember our future without Sankofa sensibilities. For a marvelous future to emerge, the best of ancestral wisdom and energy must be present and palpable. Sankofa teaches us that there is no way forward that does not look to the past. And the past is not a philosophical construct. The past is the people who came before us. The past is the ancestors.

The United States of America is on a collision course with a violent end because it looks back to an ahistorical, bleached past that causes it to go forward without having learned from its sins. America is a bird that does not fly forward, but flies in circles. Problems many thought to be solved in America emerge—circle—again and again and again. Until we understand that even this fatigue-inducing reality is designed, we will keep going nowhere fast, together. Going in circles is our collective lot until redesign is prioritized.

If this feels like too much. It should. This is *we* work, not *me* work. We must realize that our sociopolitical outcomes, as ugly and as oppressive as many of them are, are of human design. As they were designed, they can be undesigned and redesigned. Do not believe the preachers. Our world *can* be redesigned theologically. Do not believe the politicians. Our world *can* be redesigned politically. Do not believe the CEOs.

Our world *can* be redesigned economically. It must be. Now is the time.

The work of making the world more joyful and just is our collective work. It cannot be outsourced to others. We cannot scour the globe to find people whose brutal economic realities force them to do our work of justice more cheaply. This work is yours. This work is mine. Our work begins in our bodies and spirits as they yearn for more for humanity and creation. This yearning is in so many of us who know that we are called, compelled, and seduced to create something more for ourselves and our progeny. Listen to the yearning. Listen to Spirit. Attend to the yearning. Attend to the voice. We must have the courage and the love of self to act upon what we hear.

* * *

My work here is the result of my finally yielding to a yearning, a calling that I could no longer resist and remain healthy in body and spirit. That yearning, sourced by the Divine and by ancestors has taken me to wonderful places and has facilitated encounters with extraordinary human beings, including Dr. Frances Cress Welsing.

The great psychiatrist Frances Cress Welsing is now an ancestor. Her work fed the artists that fed my soul. The poets who planted hip-hop in my soul extolled her book *The Isis Papers*. Dr. Welsing was unyielding in her commitment to Black psychological and physical liberation from internalized oppression. *The Isis Papers* was the book that everyone pretended to have read to maintain credibility in my social circle. At the time it was released, I didn't read all of it, but I sure as hell talked like I had. I had no idea that my life would intersect with Dr. Welsing's in a most significant way.

The intersections, crossroads, and happy surprises of life find us in the very places and among the very people who have motivated and challenged us. When I am practicing prayer and attentive to the swirlings of spirit and life all around me, I am aware that the Divine and the ancestors immerse me in wonderful waters. The marvelous still manages to dance upon the murderous landscapes of America. I pause to take it in. And words come to me that demand to be written and spoken. Ideas for communities I serve like Metropolitan come fast and furiously. These ideas want to be tested and seem to help move me and the people I serve forward as we explore organizational questions and solve institutional problems.

The Divine sings lyrics perfectly crafted for the music of the universe. We are called to design the space where hearing this sacred song is possible.

I know when I am hearing that music. It was music I heard clearly when I had the privilege to meet Dr. Welsing as she did her work in and around Howard University. I had a face-to-face meeting with the one who inspired my inspirers. I was fanboying and I was hoping she wouldn't pick up on it. But, hey, she was a psychiatrist. When I met her, Dr. Welsing was a regal elder. She was striking. She was statuesque. Her crown of an Afro radiated power and prescience and made my body want to bend in honor and respect. Her knowing energy permeated the room and went through me like radio waves. A no bullshit forcefield enveloped her. I don't remember much about our conversation. I do remember my gratitude for being in her presence and telling her so.

Not long after our meeting, Dr. Welsing died. Her community searched for a place to celebrate her life and ancestral ascendance. They asked if Metropolitan would host. Of course I said yes. We met and planned for a large crowd. Media would be present. It was going to be a celebration fit for the queen that Frances Cress Welsing was. From the opening drums to the libations poured to the reflections upon her life by those who knew and loved her, it would be a luminous gathering.

There was one wrinkle, however. As we planned, I noticed tension. You've felt this before. You know the energy that fills a room when someone wants to ask a question they are petrified to ask. There was a halting spirit emanating from a few folks. I felt it. And I waited.

"Pastor," they said, "we have a question. May we build an ancestral altar honoring Dr. Welsing in Metropolitan's sanctuary?" It was a big question to be sure. Ancestral altars contain photographs, symbols, foods, and items meaningful and sacred to the living dead and to us. For many reasons, I responded, yes. I knew that they had heard from Christian churches and preachers before. I knew that my kind had denigrated this practice before out of ignorance and self-hate, the very kind of self-hate that Frances Cress Welsing labored to eradicate.

I also knew that my ancestors had built ancestral altars for millennia before they built churches. I knew that Metropolitan African Methodist Episcopal Church is both ancestral altar and ancestral shrine. The impulse to build Metropolitan was related to the impulse that led our ancestors to build altars. The table in front of the church demands that we remember. The altar that I said yes to would do the same.

The altar had to be built not only to honor Dr. Welsing, but to heal Metropolitan. We needed to embrace our knowledge of the Divine and of self that predated our journey to this place. The altar to celebrate and venerate Dr. Welsing was built and she was celebrated in good fashion, as my forebears would say.

That altar was built, and it was physically dismantled. But it remains. I can see it still. It was in front of the brass cross. It was in front of the wooden communion table that the brass cross sits atop. It was in front of the altar where we knelt to take communion before COVID changed our habits.

The altar of Frances Cress Welsing exists both within time and outside of time at Metropolitan African Methodist Episcopal Church. It exists whenever one of our beloved rests for the final time in front of cross and table. At Metropolitan, that altar has held space for Frederick Douglass, A. Philip Randolph, Rosa Parks, and Mother Mary Burroughs, our sainted church mother. Names you know and names you don't know. That altar has always reveled in Black life and marked Black death. It always will. From that very altar my journey will both end and begin again.

We are a space designed for human connection and divine awareness. We embrace our story, past, present, and future. We are not ashamed of the revolutionary gospel, nor are we ashamed of our Africanness. We design our space for all. But it looks like us. It sounds like us. And every human is welcome. We rejoice in the fact that universal humanity can be accessed through our precious particularity.

We are a people on the move. Nomadic in the truest sense. We will not stay in one place for very long according to the funeral liturgy of African Methodism. We will forever be moving across time and space. First cloaked in recognizable flesh, then cloaked in corporeal mystery. Those who move as we move must design not only homes and places of worship. We must design time so that we hear the music of the wisdom of the ages. We must design so that we may be. We must design for the eternal reality of being kinesthetic spirit-people.

There are many ways to do this. Some wear jewelry that belonged to ancestors. Some wear pendants bearing the images of saints. We pray the prayer beads and rosaries of our mothers and fathers. Others wear clothing adorned with ancestral images and symbols. We know that it is not enough to have stationary altars and sites of ancestral remembrance. We must mark our Divine and ancestral awareness as we move toward the unknown. We do not, cannot, and must not move unaccompanied by ancestors.

In Hebrew scripture the ark of the covenant is mobile ancestral awareness. The people were peripatetic. Always on the go. They set up tents and dwelled for a spell. They broke those same tents down and kept pushing forward. They could not wait to stop moving to design their space. They designed as they moved and moved with their design.

The ark was made of acacia wood and contained the two tablets of the Ten Commandments, Aaron's budding rod, and a golden urn filled with manna. This holy, rectangular chest was suspended on poles and carried by the community wherever they roamed. The ark was a Divine and ancestral presence in the camp of the people. It was always ready to move as the people moved.

By design, the people had the Divine and the ancestral at the center of their lives and movements. So must we. The people carried the commandments in the ark to remind themselves that they were in relationship with the Divine, always and everywhere. May we design to remember the same. The people journeyed with Aaron's budding rod to remind themselves of the priestly function not only of one family, but of all the families of the earth. We must be awakened to the human vocation of representing the Divine in all that we say and do.

Each human action is theological because we embody divinity. May we design to remember this truth. The people had a golden urn filled with manna. We must always remember that provision of the Divine. As our ancestors were nourished, so shall we be nourished. And those who come after will know that same provision.

Let us design internally and externally. Let us design knowing that every space is curated to produce outcomes. We design ancestrally to produce beauty, joy, and liberation.

9

The Ancestral Guides We Need

WE ARE ALL ancestor venerators. Our bodies, homes, and places of work and worship all say so. The names of our nations, states, counties, and cities say so. Our public buildings and spaces say so. Our world is filled with the energy of the living dead. It seems to have always been this way. I think it always will be. Even our names are ancestral energy.

And lurking beneath the bread and circuses, something at work beyond politics and chicanery, beyond the stubbornness of America to do what is right and just for all people, are the shadow ancestors who persist. Their strong energy is a catalyst for this work. The masses being suckered by visual and rhetorical shell games points to a deeper malady than can't be explained by the usual suspects on the Sunday morning political shows. Journalists, scholars, and politicians do not have the language to shine a light on every facet of the intractability of injustice in America. Shadow ancestral energy is at work, being manipulated to keep the language of freedom ringing while political and economic bondage persist.

Some only name as ancestor those whose lives were beneficent and benevolent. I extend to shadow ancestors the same designation. Their malevolent power among us persists and their progeny know this. We did not create that energy, and we cannot destroy it. Some believe it can be redeemed. I think it wiser to be always ready to fight it and know that it specializes in shapeshifting and "playing possum." The very moment you believe that the shadow ancestral energy of colonialism, voter suppression, segregation, or lynching is asleep it hisses and shows its teeth. And it will bite.

In our day, shadow energy persists as people no longer employ conceits to hide their intentions of injustice. They say what they want to say. And they say it with their chests. Take them at their word, no matter how diabolical, despicable, and dumb they sound.

I choose to venerate ancestors who chose to be human. I choose those who did not make peace with violence, oppression, exploitation, and imperialism as did the founders of the United States of America. These human ancestors are most worthy of remembrance and honor. Many of the living dead thrust upon us by schools, houses of worship, and civil society did not center the well-being of all, but of some. They were unwilling to extend liberty and abundance to every precious human being. They made excuses for systems that delivered pain and death domestically and globally. These people must be remembered for their abandonment of what it means to be fully human—human, meaning, to ensure the liberation of all from every conceivable bondage.

These shadow ancestors must be remembered. They must not be venerated.

The problems that face us daily have roots deeper than the visible issues that assail and assault us. Electing the right people may help some, but the issues seem to return like waves crashing upon the shore. Kumbaya signs of togetherness and embracing one another across racial, religious, and economic lines are good for optics and social media, but don't solve much. Our well-buried problem is identification. Most of us do not actively identify with the living dead among us who point us in the direction of liberation.

We will never be free by venerating American presidents who have made peace with the bloodiness of American empire and preachers who have added the blood of Christ to the blood of Indigenous peoples and Africans and the poor and the disregarded from every culture. We will never be free by venerating titans of industry who have made their wealth by crushing workers and extracting and commodifying the earth's good gifts while tossing us coins and calling it philanthropy.

Remember these politicians, preachers, and businessmen. Study their lives. And then scream, "Hell no!"

Decide to live for another. Decide to live for the planet, not the nation state. Decide that peace among humankind is worth living for, fighting for, and dying for.

* * *

I remember one particular event like it was yesterday. It was within the time my father was employed by State Farm Insurance, from 1972 until 2010. He was one of the first Black men hired by the company's Southeast Region. Daddy was a handsome and thin, dark and determined young man. He had a gleaming smile and an Ebony and Jet magazine-ready Afro. Photographs of him from that era exude power rooted in joy and an awareness that the mountain before him would not defeat him.

State Farm had a corporate "family ethos" and often included the children of employees in essay contests and things of that ilk. I entered an essay contest in about 1982 or 1983, before my tenth birthday at the urging of Daddy and Momma, who always encouraged my thinking, reading, and writing. Always.

It was a July 4 essay contest. You know the drill. Steroidal American propaganda and nostalgia. As uncritical as parents staring at their newborn child. All lights, balloons, and unicorns. Contestants were asked to write about a great American president, as I recall. I still don't know why I chose to write about Dwight David Eisenhower. Was his name stuck in my little head because the Eisenhower Parkway was a major thoroughfare in Macon, Georgia? We traveled that big road every day on the way to Saint Peter Claver Catholic School. Was it the image of his face in our classrooms? Maybe that was the connection.

If you are of a certain age, you were in a similar classroom. Presidential photographs from George Washington to Ronald Reagan adorned the wall. The wall dripped with white male hegemony and testosterone. What were we to do other than be mystified by the images of these living dead? Our little desks of wood and steel were like altars and all around were presidents. Maybe I could grow up and be one?

My classroom was designed for ancestral veneration of the men who occupied the White House. Most of them were committed to white domination at home and racialized American imperialism abroad. From within that milieu, I wrote about Eisenhower as the greatest American president. There was no criticism in my little essay. And none would have been accepted by the judges of the contest. The purpose was celebration of American greatness through American presidents. Period. Cue Kool and the Gang.

The places where I learned and played were not designed to elicit questions from me. They were not designed for me to ask why Macon, Georgia, has the Ocmulgee Mounds but precious few Indigenous people. I was not encouraged to ask why the city was ordered racially and economically as it was. I was trained to be pliant and productive. To put my head down and play by the rules. To do my part to keep the diesel engines of American empire on track.

But there was always fugitivity in our Black existence. I was encouraged also by family and community to read, think, write, and speak. The beautiful womb of Blackness I knew as a child nourished us with quiet yet palpable waters of resistance. In the words of Muddy Waters, I am a full-grown man. Yet, the umbilical cord that supplies ancestral and spiritual nourishment has never been cut. Praise G-d.

We were taught to notice when the American Imperial Express rolled over human lives and derailed dreams. And we were taught in the school of our elders and parents that that was not the will of G-d. We were taught to go to church, pray, and "get our lesson" so that we could do something about it.

The essay contest topic was limited to presidents. To white men. Would I have chosen differently if the options were expanded? Eisenhower built on Truman's work and helped to desegregate the military, after being pushed by organized Black power and its allies. No small feat politically. But he needed soldiers, sailors, and marines for the work of empire. Gestures and opportunities abounded. But what about real justice for all? Incrementalism, poisonous and powerful, remains the sickening order of the day.

We are surrounded by powerful images of American godliness and goodness. Where those we are taught to venerate saw imperfections in the American imperial experiment, they were satisfied to tweak around the edges of death and unwilling to promote and build a system dedicated to life and liberation for all.

I almost became a satisfied person. This satisfaction takes different forms. It can be being okay with the world as it is. It can be a nihilistic resignation that things cannot change. It can be a tepid response of feeling awful about present conditions but unwilling to join those doing something to create change. A satisfied person is a dead person.

Remember this: A just political order is as possible as our present unjust order. The forces arrayed against this are myriad and powerful, but the joyful, human fight against them is our calling and our destiny. The soaring poetry of my faith tradition, given to me by my ancestors, is rooted and grounded not in death, but resurrection. Ancestors would not let me be satisfied. They would not let me die the death of satisfaction.

In 1948, Muddy Waters recorded the song "I Can't Be Satisfied." I listened to that song again and again. The tinny sound quality could not squelch the plaintive, yet jaunty energy of Muddy's vocals. He sounds like he is trying to rise from the fertile muck of the Mississippi Delta and build a world where the love he seeks is the love he gets. His unrequited love is reminiscent of my people's sojourn here. We have loved America with body and blood. We have been more loyal than any group. Yet, the one we have tried to love brings trouble to most of us and causes us to "be all worried in mind." Muddy asks his beloved to come with him. Muddy contemplates violence. Muddy cries.

The soil that produced Muddy and his music was the sight of the wedding of Black genius and Black suffering. Muddy chants the sacred incantation that holds the key to liberation, "Well babe, I can't never be satisfied." This is the mantra of ancestors of light and those who would take up their ongoing work in our world. We must not be satisfied with ourselves as we are. We must ever evolve from glory to glory. Muddy sings, "I be troubled. I be all worried in my mind.

Well, honey, ain't no way in the world for me to be satisfied. And I just can't keep from crying." The refusal to be satisfied is answered prayer. The tears water our wonderful next.

This capitalist system offers toys of distraction to us. Access to power, grants, degrees, vacations, lectures, sermons, honoraria. All things that can be used for good. But things that must remain in service of liberation. Achieving them is never the goal itself. Churches, sermons, and denominations can obscure, if not altogether obliterate, how Spirit is moving and how we are being summoned and seduced to join her revolution. So much of our world and so many of our institutions are designed to tame us, distract us, and silence us. Ancestors of light, however, keep us on the journey toward the bright sunrise of human flourishing and unmitigated joy.

We settle for so little here. The wealth needed to alleviate poverty is in our hands. The creativity needed to bury this unjust order so that a just one may rise resides in our beautiful bodies and our fathomless souls. The strength we need lives in our every sinew. The courage we need breathes in our collective commitment. Together, we must take what my friend Stephen Lewis calls "the next faithful step."

There are ancestors that show us a more excellent way. They have radiant layers of depth that reveal our own. The closer we journey with them, the more they allow the light of truth to flood our souls and illumine the path we must take if we would be free.

The first ancestor beyond blood ties to seize me was Martin Luther King Jr. He was born in a city I knew well. Riding from Macon to Atlanta in the plush backseat of my grandfather's Pontiac Bonneville to visit my father's sister was a highlight of my young life. A trail of Lamar cars would book up I-75 headed north for fellowship and fun. It was life giving. And so was learning all I possibly could about Dr. King.

He was a preacher. I, too, was seduced from an early age by the sounds, sights, and soulfulness of the church. His image was ubiquitous. Little Black boys who grew up in my era saw King's face on calendars given to clients by Black banks, insurance companies, and funeral homes and on fans that (kind of) kept us cool when hot, humid Georgia summers slapped us in sanctuaries. His image also beatifically dwelled on commemorative plates in almost every Black Southern household, next to plates bearing the likenesses of white Jesus and John Fitzgerald Kennedy.

I knew his voice and his speeches. His mellifluous baritone, seasoned by cigarette smoking, compelled me. I was very young, but in some way, I understood his commitment to liberation and justice. We sang about him in school. We fought for his birthday to become a federal holiday. We committed to memory stirring snippets from "I Have a Dream." I kept a picture of him in the bedroom I shared with my little brother. I fanned the flame of his ancestral energy that resided in my heart. He was a model for me—young, gifted, Black, eloquent, determined, and charismatic. He was for me an ancestral frontiersman, beckoning me to build new heavens and new earths.

I wanted to be like him. I was glued to every documentary about King and the civil rights movement of the 1950s and 1960s. The sounds and images mesmerized me. One minute singing and preaching, which I knew well. The next minute, forces of violence arrayed against my people, materializing as barking dogs, bullets, nooses, and billy clubs deployed to break their bodies and their spirits. I wanted to be there with them. I felt as one born out of time. Like I should have come to this plane of existence in that generation and not my own. My arrival in 1974 had to be the result of some worrisome wrinkle in the space-time continuum.

I held on to the feeling that my world would be better if I found a way to live in my generation like Martin Luther King Jr. lived in his. My family blessed my curiosity. They took me to every King memorial march, prayer breakfast, and worship service within driving distance. I was disciple, acolyte, and fan.

My aunt and uncle purchased Taylor Branch's biography of King for me when I was quite young. It waited for me until I was mature enough to deal with its literal and metaphorical weight. And that's how it happened. I grew to understand who this man was slowly. To understand that he came from a familial and cultural background of disruption, pride, and protest. I grew to understand that we remember his name, but he was only one of many who demanded to be treated as human with unmatched dignity and strategic aplomb.

Unfortunately, the statist interpretation of Martin Luther King Jr. reigns in our day. Out of context snippets of his powerful rhetoric are used not to transform us, but to paint an untrue portrait of linear and evergreen American progress toward justice. We have been given a King fit for broad, uncritical consumption.

The King we get isn't at all like the King who lived, was executed, and keeps rising again and again.

Corporate America, political parties, and government give us the "content of your character, not the color of your skin," King. This is the MLK that white supremacists give us to prove that white supremacy no longer exists. They pretend that the violent, racialized political economy of their ancestors has been long since supplanted by meritocracy. Everyone who works hard and plays by the rules has the same shot at succeeding. King is now avatar for post-racial America, and, intentionally taken out of context, King's words are given to us meaning whatever a corporate or government comms shop wants them to mean. Their newly extracted meaning is as far from King's intention as the east is from the west.

King and the ancestral forebears who gave him eyes to see and ears to hear labored to build a world where character drove outcome for all people. But that could only happen when the belief system that ensured that white people mattered more was utterly destroyed. He never meant to say that we already live in a world where character matters more than skin color. He was saying that we are going to organize and fight until that world emerges. That world eludes and evades us still.

King brilliantly leveraged the language of this nation's founding documents to paint a picture of what we could be. The Declaration of Independence, the Constitution, and its Amendments were sampled by King like a masterful golden era hip-hop DJ. The best DJs found break beats and stretched them for the purpose of the collective movement of bodies. King found beautiful words and phrases that America wrote and spoke but refused to embody. King knew that only a new song could make flourishing possible, and he used the old music as foundation for the new. His music was the soundtrack that inspired movement.

The King given us by the national holiday firmly believes in American exceptionalism. Each January, we are offered by churches, oligarchs, and plutocrats a Martin Luther King Jr. who has the characteristics of a deep fake. It looks like MLK. Sounds like MLK. But the words are used to cheerlead the status quo, sanitize the past, and excuse the ongoing workings of oppression. King looms large in our collective memory. His spirit was too large, his words too potent, and his death was too violent to forget. For now. Therefore, for the purposes of the American imperium, King, the revolutionary, required an extreme makeover. We now have a bespoke King, tailored for American amnesia, self-congratulation, and commerce.

But for those who would stop, look, and listen, there still exists the King whose last sermon, which he did not live to preach, was going to be titled "Why America May Go to Hell." This same preacher said in "Beyond Vietnam: A Time to Break Silence," that "America was the greatest purveyor of violence in the world." He spoke against the triple evils of racism, militarism, and the poverty wrought by capitalism. There was a crystal-clear reason why FBI leadership labeled him "the most dangerous man in America."

I am frustrated that we are not given a more honest picture of the man. But we cannot expect that from corporations. We cannot expect that from government. And we cannot expect that from the imperially captured American church. The information-industrial complex that manipulates what we see and hear has no interest in the revolutionary ideas that resulted in King's execution. They do not want school children, motivated by MLK's ongoing ancestral energy, to be trained to ask why things are as they are. They do not want adults, under King's influence, who break free of the duopoly of imperial religion and politics that distort our minds, render impotent our dreams, and make us sycophants of a brutal capitalist world order.

If King were the person who governments, corporations, and churches claim he was, he would either still be alive or he would have died of old age. If he had been useful to the powerful, he would not have met the fate of Christ. As the church has retrofitted Jesus Christ for Sunday consumption, King has been retrofitted for American civil religion. He has been canonized as the patron saint of post-racial America. I call bullshit.

His vision and organizing made him dangerous. His work was bequeathed to him from the Divine and from the Ancestors. He walked a trail already blazed by so many. And he did not walk alone. King the disrupter walks among us. Hidden in plain sight. In books. In videos catalogued on social media. The King of high school assemblies and prayer breakfasts encourages us to do good as milquetoast community service. The living dead Martin Luther King Jr. calls for nothing short of a spiritual, theological, economic, and political revolution.

The ancestral guides we need move us beyond where we are. MLK was there waiting for me to awaken to my passion and purpose. Ancestors are waiting for your awakening, too. He challenged me to never go to another civic meeting and pray prayers that make Democrats and Republicans comfortable. He challenged me to view every economic policy from the vantage point of its effect upon the poorest and most vulnerable among us. He challenged me to always view oppression as global and interlocking. Racialized oppression and anti-immigrant fury in America is related to anti-immigrant fury in Europe and creeping fascism globally. Oligarchs and their elected lickspittles know that they can maintain power by stirring up white demographic anxiety and turning it into votes whipped by their potent media echo chambers.

King tied racism at home to the Vietnam War abroad. We must tie racism at home to other territory grabbing, imperial movements veneered and strengthened by a muscular civil religion that claims G-d's desire is for the glorious return of the Russian Empire. The state's best concealer for a non–critical thinking populace is G-d language. But King's use of G-d language was steeped in a recognition of a human family that defied borders. In America today G-d is the uncritical national deity of the American empire. Not the Creator of the universe. Certainly not the G-d enfleshed in Jesus Christ.

The violent geopolitical winds now blowing do not recognize the fiction of borders. We live in a "World House," King wrote. His ancestral light shone bright enough for me to look beyond what those interested in exploiting his legacy said about him. Reading King's words and immersing myself in the work of trustworthy interpreters of his life and ministry connected me to his radical and revolutionary praxis. King was not perfect, but he had the courage to preach and act beyond restrictive dogma and doctrine that often acts to protect the church from getting blood on its shirt and mud on its shoes. King connected the pain of his people with the pain of all people. And he moved to the music of liberation until met by balcony's bullet. No matter how hard they try with holidays and sleight of hand he won't stay dead.

The ancestral guides we need were not maintenance persons. They were architects and builders. They imagined. They designed. They built. They composed songs that live in our bodies and spirits, which we have yet to sing. They wrote sublime freedom symphonies, and we have not taken our instruments out of their cases to play the music. Like masters of jazz, even their off-notes were folded into songs that move bodies and souls. Now is the time to sing. Now is the time to play. The ancestors we need were tuned to the frequencies of the universe. The Divine showed them the dream written in star and stream, in the beauty of the lilies and the bodies of each human to ever inhale oxygen and exhale carbon dioxide. That dream is the liberation of all creatures so that they can thrive in community without encumbrance or exploitation.

We can center love instead of hate. We can create economies that meet human needs without producing crippling poverty and pornographic wealth. We must transfer wealth from the few to the many. Why are people struggling for food, shelter, and safety when billionaires are being produced by the same system? We are aching for what belongs to us all. What belongs to us all is being controlled by a few. This injustice will not stand.

The work of poet Seamus Heaney resounds. Especially "The Cure at Troy." We suffer. We torture one another. We get hurt. We get hard. Is a further shore reachable from here? Dare we believe in miracle? In cures and healing wells? It is so difficult to believe. Hope can seem an assent to deception. But only a sweaty, sinewy hope that bends the moral arc of the universe toward justice will do. Hope sure as hell ain't waiting for G-d or people to do the work that we must do. When I want to give up, the ancestors won't allow it. They continuously light the path to the marvelous in our murderous reality without diminishing the horror we see or silencing the cries we hear.

We are defined by the narratives to which we cling. Those who seek to free us from the dangerous fictions of our defining mythologies are doing the most difficult work that humans can do. Those called to change our stories so that our behavior changes stir up fear and violence. My ancestor's vision for life in this nation was as old as human thought itself. Freedom, charity, and community for all. Nothing more. Nothing less. This dream was not shared by the small people who ruled this land stolen by violence. They believed that power grows only when hoarded, not when it is shared. And their ideological children continue to strangle us.

The weapon they use against these story-changers is always death. Not only are shadow ancestors and their progeny destruction seekers, but these people are also not very creative. They use the same means generation upon generation. Crucifixion. Lynching. Assassination. Prison. Lack of universal health care. Lack of fair wages. Be it fast death or slow death, it's all death. But death doesn't stop story-changers. Story-changers don't stop speaking. Their poetry does not disappear. Their work of exorcism continues. They cast out stories of death for stories of light, life, and love and the reality of resurrection. These ancestors burst out of tombs every day.

The Spirit that drove their work cannot be conquered or killed. Humans have mastered the technologies of death. But love, laughter and the desire for liberation that lurks in every human heart cannot be killed. The ancestral guides we need defy crucifixion, execution, and assassination. They fan sparks of light and love into flames that cannot be extinguished.

The sparks are all around us. People are organizing, planning, writing, praying, laughing, loving, and dancing into newness. Sparks abound. What the world needs now is conflagration. We must be on fire with revolutionary love that abandons sentimentality and establishes justice nourished by peace.

Ancestral guides are still finding us. Their true energy, not manipulated by marketers and statecraft, can be found in the work of serious craft and scholarship. Some of our most reliable ancestral connectors are scholars committed to unearthing truths the powerful would prefer to be forgotten. Ancestral guides are also finding us in music, poetry, paintings, sculpture, silence, and dance. Freedom lovers and freedom seekers find each other. Time, space, even death cannot stop their coming together. The mysterious Source that inspired those who came before us beckons us to join the work of creation and to pass that work to those to come. Source is not just beckoning us to work. Source desires us, will fill us, and set us on journeys to discover our specific roles in building thriving human communities that care for all of creation.

What ancestors have found you? They may be obscure. They may not be the subjects of books, articles, documentaries, or lesson plans. But they are hovering and sweeping and speaking. Their stories are searching for you. Put yourself in a position to be found. Listen. Be open. Be curious. Read. Be still. Listen for them. Go to lectures. Listen for names and narratives that pierce you and won't leave you alone.

Research those names. Plunge into those lives. I recall as a child, I would only read biographies. I thought fiction was a waste of time. I was wrong. Very wrong. But my commitment was to dive into the lives of those who had come before me. I wanted to learn, grow, and be inspired and caught up in the mystery that allows the living dead to shape and mold the living. They were us. We are them. And we will soon occupy the plane where they dwell.

The ancestral guides we need are seers in a world of denial. Our world is filled with people who pretend not to see human pain immediately before them. Our world is teeming with people who pretend not to hear the screams of human misery all around them. But seers discern what is unfolding before their eyes. They cannot proceed with business as usual. They tell the world what they have seen. They shout it from rooftops. They cannot not see. They cannot keep what they have witnessed to themselves. They will not rest until others also bear witness to that which diminishes our siblings' human potential.

Seers see where we are and where we can go. They are possessed by visions of a new world dawning with precious possibilities for all humankind. The ancestral guides we need are seers in a world where the powerful use distraction and denial to keep us indifferent, disconnected, and dreamless.

You've heard it before. The opposite of love is not hate. It is indifference, that cold, avoidant impulse unmoved by the myriad difficulties faced by our human and creaturely kin. Indifference to ecological devastation, poverty, and the material deprivation of large swaths of the globe is commonplace in our time. This indifference is not just misanthropic, it is murderous. It intensifies the energy of death as it marches across the earth. Our collective lack of action hastens the demise of many.

The ancestral guides we need are not indifferent. They are artisans creating a hopeful future using the tool of active, sweaty love. They call us to the same creative work of love. We are called to a love that sees and hears. To a love that is risky within a denial-filled world. We are called to a love that feeds souls and bodies. We are called to love that sacrifices comfort in the interest of caring for the needs of others. This is the love the ancestors embody that wants to emerge in us, robust and palpable.

The ancestors who seize me day by day shine light on a path that leads us to humanity and love. For some time now I have searched for a different way to say this. *Humanity* and *love* seem like weak words given the cacophony of effective, deceptive speech swirling around us. Not so. There are no stronger words. Humanity and love are the building blocks for the revolution to come. That revolution will build systems, economies, politics, and theologies that do not exploit or scapegoat. The ancestors call us to join the revolution.